ARROW
Countdown

REBUILDING A DREAM AND A NATION

Peter Zuuring

Kingston, Ontario - 2001

Arrow Countdown 09
Rebuilding a Dream and a Nation

Copyright© 2001, Arrow Alliance Press

Canadian Cataloging in Publication Data

ISBN 1-55056-866-3

Main entry under title:

Arrow Countdown 09:
Rebuilding a Dream and a Nation

      Includes index.
      ISBN 1-55056-866-3
      1. Arrow...Aviation
      2. Rebuilding...History, Canada

First Printing, November 2001

Design by Peter Zuuring & Jozef VanVeenen
Typesetting and Layout by Jozef VanVeenen
Cover Design - Jozef VanVeenen
Photo Editing/Retouching - Jozef VanVeenen
Editing - David Caple
      Essence Communications
      Lynn Macnab
      Mark Pavilons
Printed and Bound in Canada by Friesens

The Arrow Alliance has striven for content accuracy and validity. Picture credits are only given for actual photography supplied to the Alliance by individuals or organizations not part of Avro Aircraft Ltd. or Orenda engines Ltd. All photos acquired through others without a source photographer named and validated are marked "Anon." All photos, drawings, reports, etc. which are clearly Avro/Orenda in origin are just marked 'Avro' or 'Orenda' as the case may be due to the impossibility of determining, today, the actual person who took the photo. The clear photographic/ compositional skill of Lou Wise and his photo team at Avro continue to thrill me and the thousands of Arrow enthusiasts from all over Canada and beyond. We are thankful that so many pictures have survived. The Arrow story continues to twist and shout. The volume of material continues to grow. We do make mistakes. Any corrections, errors and omissions are clearly regrettable and, if informed, the Alliance will make the changes in the next printing.

Contact Us
62 North Street,

Kingston, Ontario K7K 1J8

Phone/Fax: (613) 531-4156

Direct E-mail: arrowz@attcanada.ca

Web E-mail: director@arrow-alliance.com

Website: arrow-alliance.com

Cover Story

The front cover shows the supersonic Arrow, shock waves and all, blasting through Canada's upper atmosphere. No Canadian designed/built plane has ever gone faster.

The side-view artwork was created by R. Beausart, with permission from the National Aviation Museum. It was corrected by Joe Van Veenen and Peter Zuuring.

The shadowgraphy was found in a DND, DRB, Carde experimental report, "Arrow Ballistic Range Tests of the CF-105" by H.R. Warren and B. Cheers, dated November, 1959.

The airspeed indicator drawing and function were obtained from the Arrow Mk-I service manual. The readings on the instrument correspond to actual flying conditions as outlined in the flight envelope

diagram included. An indicated airspeed of 360 knots (RAM air pressure on the nose pitot tube probe corresponds to a ground speed of Mach 1.4, at 44,000 feet above sea-level.)

The rear cover shows "Spud" Potocki climbing down from the last manufactured Arrow to fly, RL205, for less than an hour after its pristine manufacture to its disgraceful cut-up. The GENTEX H4 helmet was actually used in the fifties. The inner helmet and oxygen mask correspond. Much appreciated restoration through Gentex and their Canadian agent John Winship of Kingston, Ontario.

Open front and back reads 2009, the year of the hundredth anniversary.

Mach/Airspeed Indicator

The Mach/Airspeed Indicator located on the main instrument panel in the front cockpit displays indicated airspeed and mach number on a single dial, and the maximum allowable indicated airspeed for all altitudes. A control is provided to adjust an airspeed index, which can be set to indicate landing or take-off speed.

The instrument consists of the following three independent mechanisms:

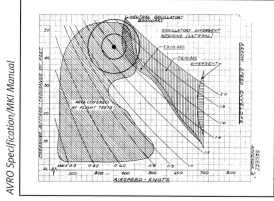

AVRO Specification/MKI Manual

(a) A pitot-static operated airspeed mechanism which drives a pointer and a pointer mask to indicate airspeed on the perimeter of a fixed dial. The dial is graduated from 80 to 850 knots; in 10 knot increments from 80 to 400 knots and in 50 knot increments from 400 to 850 knots.

(b) A static pressure operated altitude mechanism which drives a moving scale graduated to indicate mach numbers from 0.5 to 2.2 mach. The indicated mach number appears in a cutaway portion of the airspeed pointer mask. The airspeed pointer is split to indicate mach number on the inner scale and equivalent indicated airspeed on the outer scale. The mach number scale is graduated in divisions of 0.02 from 0.5 to 1.0 mach, and in divisions of 0.05 from 1.0 to 2.2 mach. The mach number scale rotates as altitude changes so that the mach number corresponds to the indicated airspeed at all altitudes.

(c) A static pressure operated altitude mechanism which drives a red and black striped pointer to indicate maximum allowable airspeed at all altitudes. The pointer is adjusted at standard sea level condition to a preset value by an adjusting screw in the rear of the case. The screw is accessible through the static pressure inlet.

A SET INDEX knob located on the lower right hand side of the bezel is used to set the airspeed index, which is a white triangular marker on the perimeter of the airspeed scale.

The altitude range of the instrument is from minus 1000 to plus 80,000 feet.

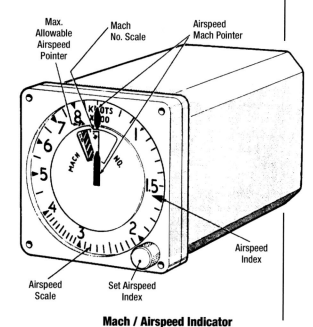

Mach / Airspeed Indicator

1

Arrow RL-201 taking off from Malton in the spring of 1958 on 32, heading north. Note the stiffness of the wings and the effortless flight the photo conveys. This flight will be repeated February 23, 2009. Will you be there?

AVRO Photo

In Appreciation of an...

On-going regard for the creativity, enthusiasm, dedication and camaraderie of the people who worked on the Avro Arrow.

And..

An example and inspiration to all Canadians.
For young Canadians especially, a model to follow, building a passion for initiative, excellence and accomplishment.

Introduction

We are embarking on a journey like no other ever undertaken in Canadian history. We, not faint of heart, can prepare ourselves for a journey that will test our limits. Setbacks and disbelief will accompany our course. Resourcefulness, perseverance and persuasion will be our answer. We can and will reach our goal!

The author with Jan Zurakowski at Kartuzy Lodge, near Barry's Bay. The Arrow has touched many lives. Jan graciously boosts the incredible achievement of those who gathered in Malton during the fifties to build, what is still today, Canada's most famous airplane.

Barry's Bay Weekly Photo

We are going to rebuild the Avro Arrow, to grace our skies once again, to celebrate the 100th anniversary of powered Canadian flight on February 23, 2009. Along the way, we will set up a process to stimulate our youth into action to better themselves and our country through a self-perpetuating process. Arrow Countdown is the vehicle which will monitor our progress and keep you, the reader, informed as we open up the road ahead.

Since publishing the Alliance's Arrow Scrapbook two years ago, thousands of Canadians have purchased and read the Arrow story. We now know that poor working relations between the RCAF and A.V. Roe Canada Ltd., a naive and inept government

and, a compliant populace, formed the basis for the Arrow tragedy. It was a Canadian story from beginning to end. (The traditional tale of US pressure on an ignorant Prime Minister to get out of their turf just doesn't hold up to scrutiny.) Let us now put behind us the fact that it did happen. Let us channel our energy into bringing the Arrow back, for our pleasure and our future.

The Arrow was a symbol of technical competence and prestige. Now it will be a symbol of renewal, a taking back of responsibility for our own future through ourselves. Our institutions' capacity, motives, and delivery have been shown to be questionable. Outside influences appear to be getting control of our country. How will we get back on track to become

Official Crest of the 50th Anniversary celebration. It was offered as a sticker to be placed on Avro/Orenda employee car windscreens. Available as a peel off in the January 30, 1959 issue of Avro Newsmagazine.

a truly "Just Society" as was so eloquently presented by the Late Right Honourable Pierre Elliot Trudeau? We have some ideas. Maybe you do too! Rebuilding the Arrow can, and will help.

Can you imagine how it felt, at the fiftieth anniversary of flight February 23, 1959, to find that the Arrow programme had been cancelled three days before? All the preparations that have been on-going are suddenly iced over as the realization sets in that Canada's greatest achievement in flight so far is no more! Dinners had been planned. Bands were to play. Speeches were to be made. Displays were to be viewed. Pride was to flow. Special stamps had been issued showing the Silver Dart to the Arrow.

How far had we come in just fifty years!

How far had we blown it in three days... incredible!

Jan tells me that Mr. McGregor, the President of Trans Canada Airlines (now Air Canada), was the key-note speaker at a CNE luncheon for the fifty year celebration. All he could speak of was about how the company was going to acquire the new DC-8 from Douglas Aircraft in the USA. Avro, you recall, had the Jetliner in 1949. What were people thinking in those days?!

We can make the 100th something to remember.

50th Anniversary planning . What was going to happen? Who was doing what? Extract from the official Avro Newsmagazine, January 30, 1959 issue.

50-Year Observance Plans Now Complete

Following is the official, now-completed, organization for the observance of this year of 1959 as the 50th year of progress and development of aviation in Canada:

The organization is headed up by a National Coordinating Council with head office in the facilities of the Canadian Aeronautical Institute at 77 Metcalfe Street, Ottawa. The Council comprises the following organizations:

  The Air Industries and Transport Association
  The Royal Canadian Air Force
  The Canadian Army
  The National Research Council
  The Canadian Aeronautical Institute
  The Royal Canadian Navy
  The Royal Canadian Flying Clubs Association
  The Air Cadet League of Canada
  The Department of Transport
  The Royal Canadian Air Force Association
  The Aviation Writers Association
  The Canadian Owners and Pilots Association

Following is the Executive Committee of the National Coordinating Council:

President: Gordon J. Stringer, Air Industries and Transport Association. **Vice-President:** Arthur H. Stewart, Air Industries and Transport Association. Roy Kervin, Aviation Writers Association. Squadron Leader Roy Wood, Department of National Defence. Wing Commander Harold Pearce, National Coordinator. **Secretary Treasurer:** H. Charles Luttman, Canadian Aeronautical Institute.

Following are some of the Chairmen of local committees across Canada from Vancouver to St. John's, Newfoundland:

TORONTO, ONT.—A/M W. A. Curtis, E.D., C.B., C.B.E., D.S.C., LL.D., A. V. Roe Canada Limited. VANCOUVER, B.C.—G. W. G. McConachie, Canadian Pacific Air Lines Limited. OTTAWA, ONT.—Charles Raymond, 1448 Woodward Avenue. LONDON, ONT.—W. E. Corfield, John Labatt Limited. WINNIPEG, MAN.—H. R. Screaton, Canadian Owners & Pilots Association. MOOSE JAW, SASK.—J. A. deRosenroll, K. J. Henderson Company Limited. CALGARY, ALTA.—A/C R. C. Gordon, Canadian Pacific Airlines. BADDECK, N.S.—D. D. B. MacLeod, Department of Highways. SYDNEY, N.S. — W. P. Sampson, 27 Howe Street.

AVRO NEWSMAGAZINE

AVRO Newsmagazine

Arrow Countdown, number 09 is the first in a series of updates.

Over the last two years, many more Arrow artifacts, photos, drawings, reports, plans, manuals etc. have surfaced. Through many Arrow Alliance presentations given, to standing room only audiences, the stories keep coming. Canadians at large appear to support the notion to rebuild the Arrow. They see the difficulties and wish us luck.

This first volume concentrates on:

What it was like to fly the Arrow? "Spud" potocki tells us. His unique writing style and flying skills had been recorded, and now reproduced, from actual flying notes and photos.

The "Human Factors" side of flying the Arrow will be explored. What science made it possible to fly at twice the speed of sound at over 50,000 feet altitude? How will the pilot know what is going on from a flying and a physiological point of view?

What can go wrong? How can the pilot do his job and get back safely? What did go wrong – an accident is investigated.

The Orenda Iroquois, developed to power the production Arrow, was considered by many to be the jewel in the crown. More details on its origins and manufacture are explored indepth. Charles Grinyer, Orenda's exacting Vice-President Engineer, tells the real story "It was a nasty business right from the beginning."

In the Arrow Scrapbook, a popular, quick read, section called "Vignettes" was much appreciated. It is repeated in Arrow Countdown featuring short interesting stories of intrigue, gossip, and fact.

Rebuilding the Arrow is one of the Alliance's goals. What has been recovered that makes this possible? Who says we can do it at all?

ATAC, (Arrow Technical Advisory Council) notes discuss these issues and show some direction. A

Dae McMillan

represent the entire MK-I service manual. A sample bulletin, covering the Para-brake, enhanced with more drawings and photos than the actual service manual, is presented.

Last year, the Arrow Alliance started talking about a cross-Canada tour of a full-scale wooden Arrow mock-up, and accompanying exhibit called Arrowmania. The need for this tour, logistics, costs, Canada-wide exposure and impact is explored.

Finally, credits and contributions for this issue are presented.

We hope you enjoy this second book, and first in a series of progress reports. Let's have your comments.

Peter Zuuring, author, Founder and first Director of the Arrow Alliance.

detailed outline of "how" we do it is presented. Samples of documents, plans, drawings, and process make it clear.

The Arrow Alliance will bring out a series of Technical Bulletins for dedicated Arrow enthusiasts. Some 60 regular issues, when complete, will

Jan Zurakowski and F/L Jack Woodman celebrate 50 years of flight with an actual size replica of the Silver Dart and a model of the Avro Arrow. This display was presented at the 1958 CNE as a prelude to the anniversary itself some 6 months later.

AVRO Photo

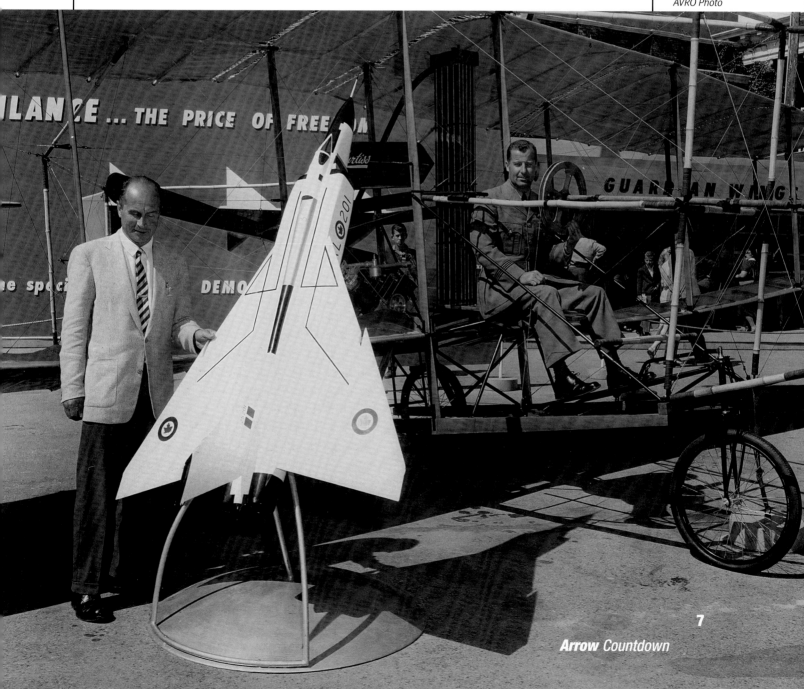

AVRO Photo

NOVEMBER 14, 1958
Vol. 4, No. 16

Avro
NEWSMAGAZINE
PUBLISHED TWICE MONTHLY BY AVRO AIRCRAFT LIMITED

Aviation Industry
Elects J. A. Morley
1959 President

Faster...
Faster...
Faster!

World's Fastest
Fighter...

At press time, the Avro Arrow,
and Chief Experimental Pilot Spud
Potocki, seen here, are subjects of
widespread international press
speculation on whether Canada
will go after the world speed record with this combination.

Avro president J. A. Plant replies
to this speculation in a statement
released Wednesday night . . .

SEE PAGE TWO

*"Spud" Potocki inviting the reader to go
for a spin. The photo was taken by Avro's
Photo Department for the cover of Avro
Newsmagazine, November 14, 1958*

Flying The Arrow

Featuring "Spud" Potocki...

"Spud" Potocki joined Avro Aircraft Ltd. in the fall of 1956. He came to Canada on the recommendation of Sir Roy Dobson. Apparently "Spud's" gift for accurately written test flight reports had brought him some recognition at Gloster Aircraft where Sir Roy was a Director. His superb flying skills, cool demeanor and years of experience no doubt added to his worth on the Arrow programme.

I have never spoken to "Spud" Potocki. Unfortunately, he died before I even got started on this project. I heard the most about "Spud" from the late Les Wilkinson, who interviewed him at length and became his friend. I have spoken at length with Jan Zurakowski and Peter Cope. I met a close personal friend of his, Elgin Scott in Rawdon, PQ. I have tried to contact his wife in Columbus, Ohio and his two step children, Michael Bridgeman and Guillian Thompson, in Ontario... but no luck. On all accounts he was liked, with a sense of humour, and respected for his professionalism. We do not intend to take away from any of the other pilots who flew the Arrow, but this section does concentrate on "Spud" Potocki. He did fly it more than anyone.

"Spud" Potocki was born Wladyslaw Potocki June, 1919 in Poland. He was five years younger than Jan Zurakowski. During the Second World War he too joined the Polish Air Force stationed, and flying with the RAF, in Britain. When Jan first met him in 1942, he was a Flt Sergeant Pilot in 306 Squadron. After the war, he continued his association with the RAF by flying for the Royal Aeronautical Establishment at Farnborough. He has taken, (successfully) the 8th sitting of the Empire Test Pilot Flight School. Just before being offered a position in Canada, he became an RAF Wing Commander and was quite comfortable in his job. Since there was a surplus of pilots after the War, he really wasn't interested in going, especially, at the salary and conditions being offered. He had flown the Gloster Javelin. With delta wing flying experience under his belt he was a fish to catch for Avro Canada, and fish they did. When he finally did agree to come on board, according to Jan, he was hired to first work with the Avrocar, flying

RL-204 lands at Trenton Air Base on February 2, 1959. A Viscount belly-landed at Malton and blocked the long north/south runway. Peter Cope landed the flight. B. Gen R.M. Cox took this photo the following morning. It was cold! "Spud" Potocki and the Arrow's ground starting equipment was flown up by Avro's DC3 transport. A little more than two weeks later, the project was cancelled. Even so, it was very well remembered in Trenton.

Avro's Flight Test Department staff on the flight line. Can you pick out "Spud" Potocki, Jan Zurakowski, Don Rogers, Peter Cope, and Mike Cooper-Slipper?

AVRO Photo

10

Arrow *Countdown*

saucer, not the Arrow. He is certainly seen flying the CF-100, and in fact is involved in the final delivery of the last CF-100 to the RCAF, as one of the photos shows.

The flying notes quoted and drawn on in this section were in the possession of Hawker Siddeley Canada. They were passed on to Les Wilkinson, by Mr. Painter, Director Corporate Affairs, to keep on behalf of the Canadian Aviation Historical Society. He was their curator/collector in the Toronto area. These notes were prepared right after each flight. Furthermore, Jan Zurakowski

confirmed that he and "Spud" would talk immediately after each flight to get their thoughts straight. "Spud" and Peter Cope prepared a pilot's transition document to pass on what it was like to fly the Arrow, it's good and bad points, and idiosyncrasies. I found it so interesting for today's reader that I have included it, in its entirety. Grammatically it does not always hang together but it is "Spud" speaking and Peter annotating. I found it interesting... I hope you do!

The notes in my possession record 8 flights only... all in October, 1958.

RCAF pilots are ready to accept into service the last MK5, CF-100, #792. "Spud" Potocki is on the far right, flanked by Don Rogers, head of Flight Test. Peter Cope, another Arrow pilot, is on the extreme left.

11

At this time Jan Zurakowski has retired as Chief Test Pilot and becomes Flight Test Staff Engineer. "Spud" Potocki takes over as Chief Test Pilot. I believe these notes represent his first month after receiving this promotion. One strange thing about the notes'; flight records indicate flight altitudes and speeds and various stick taping experiences, afterburner in and out studies, asymmetric power application and generally flying the aircraft. There is the unexpected, to be sure which dominates the flight from that point on, as shown in "Spud's" flight in RL203, when he hears and feels a banging noise and shudder through the airframe. One does not get the feeling, however, that a plan was being followed, step by step, with coordination of results and observations through chase planes or ground telemetry crews. Jack Woodman, the only RCAF pilot to fly the Arrow, speaks in Winnipeg after the demise of the programme (about the lack of planning) saying "I didn't understand it then and don't understand it today." Even so, Don Rogers, head of Avro flight test said to me over the phone that, "Planning was not always possible... every flight has its uncertainties."

Lots of time was spent in the Arrow simulator, trying to duplicate flying conditions. Apparently "Spud" was the most capable... when they first started he managed to fly it for 12 seconds before

RL201 in a steep bank, the landing gear configuration is clearly visible. "Spud" Potocki was flying the CF100 escort and getting a front row seat of the action. Hugh MacKechnie did his photo-magic with this stunning shot.

AVRO Photo

AVRO Photo

crashing. Happily, real flights were more successful. The supervisor of the Analog Simulator was Stan Kwiatkowski... you guessed it, another Pole. They look pretty intense as shown in the department photo.

It was tough to be a test pilot. You had to have guts. Imagine "Spud's" feeling as he reported during the beginning of RL203's second flight on October 1st, 1958...

"Flew 25203 - numerous snags on the aircraft, particularly bad - pedals wobbling on take-off, port throttle stuck, after-burner failed to function on selection, damper out of trim and autodamper interfering with radio...."

Then he casually says "A/C taken up to 50,000 ft. at Mach 1.7," not being fazed at all by, what anyone might call a pretty rocky take-off.

At any rate, Peter Cope told me that "Spud" was an artist of sorts in his spare time. It seems he was a bit of an artist in the air as well.

Before "Spud" got his first flight, April 23, 1958, he had to spend time on the simulator. Jan Zurakowski, with some Arrow flying experience under his belt shows "Spud" how. The simulation still left a lot to be desired. "Spud" did manage to hold the simulated aircraft steadier than any of the other test pilots albeit only for seconds!

13

October 18, 1958, RL-25203, Flight #8 "Spud" Potocki at the Controls

Perfect weather.

Took off on 32 keeping middle of the runway, dead centre, by much initial brake work. Prior to take off backlash was noted in the elevator circuit of approx. 1/3 inch, could be more. During take off slight touches of brake were used at speeds up to about 110 kts.

The run was dead straight.

The unstick was a bit fast - 170 kts. - with nose wheel coming off around 140 kts.

25203

On unstick the sideslip indicator showed 25 degrees port sideslip for balanced flight. Not much interference from lack of damper on take off, but the gear was not selected "up" until Lorne (chase plane?) has joined to checkup. Prior to this, the damper was selected to "gear-down" mode and this was later changed to "gear-up" mode. On selection there was no response from the indicator until the handle was pressed upwards.

Re-backlash in pitch increased to 1/2 inch at least from 1/3 inch reported on the ground.

After a shaky flight, RL203 makes it back to Malton. The long runway 32-14 is clearly visible below

The climb was made to 25,000 feet and aircraft stabilized at test Mach numbers.
No problem with the damper was experienced and generally, apart from last run which was on the other side of the drag curve – conditions were good.

An acceleration past Mach 1.1 was made on the climb to 42,000 feet with intention of gaining 50,000 feet at 1.1 MN. Prior to this, serious fluctuations were experienced with pressurization

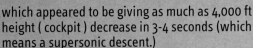

which appeared to be giving as much as 4,000 ft height (cockpit) decrease in 3-4 seconds (which means a supersonic descent.)

At about 42,000 and 1.15 MN, 1/2 a minute after the engines were closed with A/B operating - a loud bang and series of rapid knocks appeared, shaking the cockpit structure, particularly the floor, stirring up some dust. The A/B was pulled out immediately and a/c decelerated to subsonic conditions. Chase aircraft did not report any trouble visible from outside. An occasional knock was felt until speed was decreased to 0.64 MN at 35,000 ft when all this seemed to stop.

Re: control in pitch with the backlash, gave actually more accurate flight during consumption runs because flight was made with small friction and was often accurate to the extent that as much as 2 minutes could be flown without change in altitude of more than +/- 20 ft.

The approach was made with the damper 'gear-up' mode and no problem of alignment existed. The attempt was made to land in a straight run as accurately as possible and centre of runway was selected with the aircraft nose slightly to one side until approx. 300 ft from ground. The approach varied between 185 kts. and 175 kts. - during the final stages with aircraft nose just coming below the runway edge line. Rather rapid rate of descent resulted from partial engine closing, 3000/3000 rpm per side, - engine speed was not altered and

The aircraft stopped approx. 50 yds from gravel strip, having touched down about 300 ft from the beginning of the runway. This was the shortest but not the smoothest landing that has been made to date.

Prior to getting in to the aircraft some fouling existed near a rod of the elevator pickup - this fouling was scratched by a rubber seal and some later utility paint job used for the sealer.

The ground handling was quite good.

Approx. 3-4 minutes from the trouble reported during supersonic flight, the reheat light came on and did not leave the warning panel even after assuring ???? and after temperature control was set to off. Some cockpit warming was experienced after the trouble as reported above.

This was a part of trouble reported, a good flight and apart of some large break-out on ailerons, the controls felt quite good overall.

Re vision for navigation from 25,000 ft is poor as lots of fluid space results from the nose.

During start-up, difficulty was experienced with no engine light-up, this was probably caused by bad setting of high pressure cock.

The amber warning lights panel is useless in direct sunlight. It had to be covered with both hands to see during the trouble reported if any warning lights were coming on or not.

The experimental panel is very badly placed - so is the TFF. The later must be moved forward sooner than later.

more concentration was put to checking the aircraft in line. This was successful and gentle touchdown resulted.

The runway heading was kept well and parabrake operated by feel after the nose was lowered on the ground. The parabrake swing was guarded against, but it was not at all severe in any way. Re heading was kept with moderate braking and the centre of the runway never went outside the wheels. The tires on inspection were in good order.

AVRO Photo

RL-205
one and only flight

AVRO Photo, Jan. 11, 1959

RL-205, spooling up the engines for take-off on 32. The landscape looks as bleak as the circumstances the Arrow was to find itself in a few short weeks.

CF-105 Handling Notes

1. External Check

2. Cockpit Check

Do not strap in until leg restraint is fixed in place to satisfaction. Then carry out 1st preliminary cockpit check. Leave hood open.

2.1 All circuit breakers in. Damper switch to "ON"- IFF to "Correct"mode. UHF to correct channel but leave off. Check low pressure cocks as they often are closed and are not very well visible underneath throttle box. Crossfeed central. Damper Roll and Pitch switching to OFF (on port side of cockpit above radio). Check all fire warning and extinguisher buttons for correct setting. check all other switches on port side to ON.

2.2 Adjust rudder pedals counting the amount of notches on each for even alignment.

2.3 Check instrument panel. Set altimeter. See the A/H flag and T/S indicator flag is off. Adjust height of seat. Check STB consoles. Check all switches as per pilot's operating instructions. Particularly noting the following:

2.4 Adjust and fit dinghy holds.

2.5 Strap in.

2.6 Make connections for PG valve, with valve in hand in this order:
  - PG valve to trousers connector;
  - thick tube of PG valve to rear connector, on seat quick disconnect.

Remember that in both cases, locking action is needed and to achieve this the locking rings must be initially depressed and turned to lock. Fix the oxygen tube to connector on the disconnect panel. Make sure that the bayonet fitting is made. This is the most difficult connection of all. When both tubes fit correctly check for firm hold and oxygen flow from PG valve which should be held in hand. Get helmet. Connect mask to helmet or hard 'top' on left side only, then make the mask microphone connection. Still holding the helmet in hand make a helmet cable connection with quick connect female socket. Check that this seats properly. Connect PG valve to vest in such a way that when force loops are made, oxygen should fill the vest and should also flow from the mask audibly. Now put helmet on! Strap mask in place and do some preliminary pre-breathing to check the effort required to breathe.

Remove bottom pin from the seat and hand over to ground crew. He will show all the pins removed from back seat. Proceed with proper cockpit check-and visually, from left to right. Select COMM on mixing box.

3. Starting Up

Put master switch to "ON". STB engine first. Closing hood.

Align on the runway very carefully by going forward 20 - 30 yards dead on the straight line of the runway and slowly apply brakes until the aircraft stops without any tendency to depart from the centre. Apply pedal pressure and hold it there as parking brake may not be reliable in holding the aircraft correctly. If it slips it will be necessary to re-align the aircraft. Make final cockpit check.

Apply throttles against heavy pressure on the rudder pedals not allowing aircraft to move. At about 90% RPM, the nose of the aircraft will depress slightly as the effect of thrust is felt and if the brakes are good, they will hold max. military thrust. Release brakes evenly but only to allow the aircraft to move ahead. The moment any tendency to depart from centre is felt, apply brakes but only a small amount. The initial acceleration is not too impressive unless A/B is used. Keep that heading at all cost by small and rapid brake applications until about 80 - 100 kts. is reached. A brake correction has been made at about 110 kts., so don't worry too much about this, just keep that heading and watch the ASI.

At 130 kts. apply very gentle pull on the stick and see that nose comes up. Sometimes a bounce is experienced just after initial elevator movement. The nose of the aircraft has only to rise about 5 degrees to get take off attitude, therefore only small elevator movement is necessary to obtain this. Once the nose boom comes up to horizon, hold that attitude. Now at this stage, without AB the aircraft will ride on the wheels and if there is any tendency to depart from the precise heading, rudder bar should be used for correction, but only with care as the feel of rudder is such that will give higher responses for the same force as speed increases which is in opposition to SABRE and CF-100 feel. If the aircraft develops a small deviation from heading, accept this, provided the judgement is made correctly that the wheels will leave the deck before coming off the runway. But this can only be done just prior to unstick.

5 . Take Off

The Aircraft unsticks at about 160 - 170 kts. and must not be pulled off the runway or it will come down again on wheels as lift is lost by upward elevator deflection. After unstick, climb slowly away watching the sideslip or ball indication and correcting accordingly on rudder to eliminate sideslip. The gear must be raised before 200 kts. is attained this means steepening the attitude or slightly throttling back prior to gear-up selection. As the aircraft unsticks it will vibrate noticeably and as the gear comes up, marked directional disturbances are felt and if allowed to develop without correction by rudder, some rolling effects may follow - the lateral control being rather heavy at this speed to suppress the roll. The best thing to do after unstick is to select

4. Taxiing

Use some throttle to start going. Check brake response after moving a few yards. On taxiing, the aircraft oscillates slightly in pitch, the rudder pedals seem very springy. Do not use rudder bar to get differential braking, just gentle, but nevertheless quite determined pedal displacements. Every time the pedal is depressed more heavily, the aircraft will judder and abruptly change direction. This can often be accompanied by shaking of the airframe and general shaking of seat and rudder bar with this.

Taxi at moderate speed with practically closed throttles. Even without using brake, airframe shake may be evident. If a chance presents itself during the long taxi run, try deflecting the rudder bar without damper to see that some effect can be obtained at speeds as low as 50 kts., particularly if wind is favourable. This will also give some idea of rudder feel which is springy and rather heavy around the centre. Turning of the aircraft around is tricky even with a 200ft. wide runway and requires good judgement. Engine and brake must be used but take care not to lock the wheels as large lumps of rubber will be torn out from the tires if the bogey rotates without the wheels turning.

normal gear down damper on the trigger. This will tend to eliminate yawing tendencies.

After gear is up – vibration ceases and smooth flight begins. The elevator control is somewhat heavy as is the aileron, both break out forces being about 4 lbs. The elevator, in addition, has a steep feel slope for small control movements. The first thing to do is to trim the aircraft to fly without using force. Then select gear-up mode on the right hand switch. The sideslip elimination is very good, and once gear-up mode is selected rudder bar can be left alone. The next thing to do is to trim the aircraft with the damper to give zero sideslip either on the ball or the sideslip indicator. Then the aileron and pitch trim should be obtained. If throttling back was necessary before wheels up selection, the throttles should have been opened right up.

The air conditioning makes lots of noise in the cockpit – and as the oxygen is breathed this noise level seems to fluctuate – this is normal.

Prior to wheels locking up, the automatic brake is applied to stop wheels rotating. This results in brake pedals being pressed away from the pilot's foot and as the pedals come down there may be some rudder bar motion connected with it.

6. Climb

On the climb attain speed of approximately 300 - 350 kts. and establish climb at that speed. The view out of the aircraft on the climb is quite good and the attitude in military thrust not at all excessive. There is a noticeable lag in response on both elevators and ailerons, but this is, at present, quite normal.

When approaching height of 25,000 feet aim to hold 0.85 MN or there about or otherwise very slow climb performance will result from this, particularly if speed is allowed to fall below 0.7 MN.

7. Subsonic Flight Without the Damper

The aircraft has less directional stability than long tail arm aircraft such as Sabre or CF-100 - hence it is easier to induce sideslip. The rudder is of course the primary source of sideslip inducement but also the aileron. The aileron drag of down-going aileron creates an out of balance directional condition resulting in yaw (called *adverse aileron yaw*, as it is in direction acting against the intended turn). This is very prominent in this aircraft without the dampers and if aileron is worked fairly vigorously to maintain level flight continuous reversed sideslip will appear without actually touching the rudder. In highly swept aeroplanes the effect of sideslip always results in strong dihedral effect, that is to say – if the aircraft nose is yawed to starboard, the port wing will have a tendency to come up in a roll. This is magnified at angles of incidence or at certain mach numbers and altitudes. Sideslip due to any

AVRO Photo

cause will always result in a tendency to roll which, if suppressed by the aileron will generate more sideslip. The main object of flying the aircraft without damper is therefore to use coordination of rudder and aileron at all times if sideslip is to be kept under control. If the aircraft rolls to port due to starboard sideslip, starboard rudder and stick movement should be used to regain level flight. The main thing to remember is that accurate directional trim is essential in this type of flight. So prior to dis-engaging the dampers one should ensure that directional trim is as near as perfect.

8. Maneuvering at Subsonic Speeds

At low altitude and higher indicated airspeeds the aircraft is sensitive in pitch. Between speeds of 300 - 350 kts. the low altitude manoeuvre is quite pleasant. Below 300 kts. the elevator feel tends to heavy up noticeably but it is still quite pleasant down to 250 kts. – at high altitude due to increase in elevator angle required for manoeuvre the initial stick force appears to lighten noticeably as the stick is pulled outside the first increased force slope. As an example – 8 lbs. pull may be required for 1st 'g', this force rising to 13 lbs. to pull additional 'g' instead

Many hours are spent in the simulator, trying to handle and land the Arrow. Flying the real thing turned out to be easier. Jan is concentrating on the controls while "Spud" adjusts the damper circuit.

AVRO Photo

Chase Pilot, "Spud" Potocki reports informally to V.P. and G.M. John Plant on how the Arrow appeared to handle on first flight. Peter Cope is perfectly silhouetted in Potocki's oxygen mask.

of 16 lbs. which normally would be expected. This effect is more pronounced supersonically. For small values of 'g' however, the general decrease in sensitivity in pitch in this flight region improves the situation as much larger control displacements (hence forces) are needed for steady manoeuvre and the initial non-linearity of force with 'g' is lost in the loads necessary to hold steady 'g' value. (Approximately 40 lbs. at 1.35 MN, 3 'g' indicated, this being the maximum permissible 'g' value for supersonic flight.)

9. Subsonic Flight With Damper In Yaw Only

This is quite straight forward, particularly if the gear-up mode is engaged. Any turn in this case is automatically co-ordinated, and this results in a flight without sideslip. For the damper gear-down mode, the transient directional disturbances are well damped but in a steady turn some sideslip will be evident to the pilot (normally port sideslip in a turn to port and vice versa) and this must be eliminated by small rudder input, which should be removed once straight flight is achieved.

10. Supersonic Flight

Whilst it is possible at certain altitudes to achieve supersonic flight without afterburning, it is recommended that the A/B is used for supersonic flight. The transition from subsonic to supersonic flight is characterized by small disturbances in roll which might or might not be detected at about 0.95 MN and can be detected on instruments by a large jump in height indication (approximately 1500 feet).

Once the aircraft settles in supersonic flight, the control in pitch and roll improve markedly due to general reduction in sensitivity in control. The flight is much steadier and easier, provided the damper in yaw is used. Without the damper, sideslip will be generated with ease and must be eliminated with co-ordination of controls as previously mentioned. Past certain areas the pilot will experience utmost difficulty to fly the aircraft clean (without the damper) – therefore no clean mode is allowed without the damper unless specially briefed.

As no rolling manoeuvres have been done yet on the aircraft and no excessive manoeuvering in pitch – this at the present prohibited.

The acceleration in supersonic flight is rapid and although no trim changes accompany this – it is difficult to fly the aircraft accurately on instruments to any given precision – at first. This particularly refers to the Mach number or ASI stabilization. The deceleration from high supersonic flight is rapid if the afterburner is closed. The engine, however, should never be throttled back past 90% RPM until the speed falls off to subsonic value. Tests on the intake behaviour after rapid closing of the throttle have not been completed as yet. The airbrake supersonically does not have much effect. It must be appreciated that any turn gives increased drag and Mach number may tend to fall. Special briefing must be obtained before any appreciable 'g'' is pulled on the aircraft in excess of 1.5 indicated 'g' at high Mach numbers.

11. High Indicated Speed Flight

With increase of speed the feel of the aircraft becomes progressively more sensitive particularly in pitch axis – at 450 kts. only small stick movements may generate quite large aircraft response. The trim rate however is quite slow and should be used to get as near as possible to trimmed condition. If the aircraft is out of trim in pitch and an attempt is made to hold attitude by pressure on the stick - the steadiness of the flight will be lost because of difficulty of holding an accurate force just outside the breakout force – this may lead to pilot induced oscillations which can become severe. In this case it is advised that the stick should be left alone for the oscillations to damp out naturally – and aircraft retrimmed for further flight.

The overall damping in pitch is much lower in tail-less aircraft generally – therefore more rapid response can be anticipated. Depending on correctness of setting up of the feel unit – occasionally some small backlash in pitch axis can make accurate control difficult without the pilot in actual fact coming out of break force. This means that much lower forces on the stick can command response – being an undesirable characteristic, it must be reported after the flight.

12. Descent

Throttle back to approximately 80% RPM – extend airbrakes and descend at 0.8 - 0.9 MN. Occasionally, some intake rumble may be experienced which manifest itself in the form of high frequency vibrational noise from the sides of the cockpit.

13. Slow Speed Behaviour
With U/C Up (at max. landing weight 56,000. lbs.)

As the speed is reduced with u/c up and max. landing weight – at about 185 kts. the first indication of buffet is felt in the form of some airframe vibration. This will tend to increase in intensity from 170 kts. The aircraft has been flown at 155 kts. ASI just after take off – representing 15 degrees of incidence. Lateral behaviour becomes progressively heavier as speed is reduced (characteristic of spring feel) – because the aileron movements needed for balanced flight are more pronounced.

The control in pitch also becomes more sluggish and much attention is needed to keep accurate height by judicious throttle manipulation to maintain altitude (approximately 90% RPM are needed at 160 kts. ASI). If the power is reduced, very high rates of descent will result.

With the gear down, vibration is felt through the airframe and this is directly dependent on the airspeed. It is severe in the aircraft at 250 kts. – moderate at 200 kts. – light to moderate at 180 kts. More drag resulting from the gear requires more throttle to hold altitude. Provided the damper is used, there is no problem to fly at 170 kts. Without the damper conditions are much more difficult and particular attention must be given towards elimination of sideslip.

14. Approach and Landing

Downwind should be entered at 250 kts. – airbrake extended and speed reduced to 200 kts. ASI when the gear can be selected, down. There is very little trim change connected with gear lowering but height will be lost unless power is immediately increased for level flight. Check for correct gear indication – check with chase pilot. A wide circuit is recommended for approach. before the turn to base leg is made the damper mode gear switch should be selected to 'gear-down' mode. - on receiving green light indication, the base leg turn should be commenced. During the turn it will be necessary to coordinate the controls to eliminate any sideslip. In the 'gear-down' mode, this is purposely allowed to enable the pilot to correct for drift prior to touchdown. Quite large rudder force may be required to eliminate the sideslip.

Once a straight run is achieved it will be found that the view on approach is quite limited and therefore a very careful approach must be made.

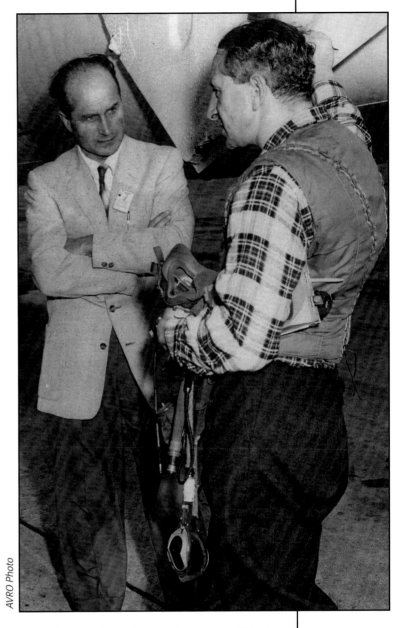

AVRO Photo

"Spud" talks to Zura after another successful test flight. Note the pressure vest that "Spud" is wearing... it makes exhaling against a pressurized oxygen source easier. Towards the middle of the flight test, programme Jan retired from active flying and "Spud" took over as chief test pilot.

The speed should be gradually reduced to 180 kts. and held there. If higher approach speeds are used, long runs result. In the case of parabrake failure it could lead to runway overrun. A cross check should also be made on the incidence indicator, alpha vane, which, at the recommended speed and max. landing weight, should register approximately 12 - 13 degrees.

The beginning of the runway should be just visible over the nose of the aircraft which for convenience may be very slightly moved to one side so that at first the runway is visible on the one side of the windscreen just outside the divider panel. This is recommended because it is felt that some

AVRO Photo

familiarization is necessary before one is fully accustomed to the use of the divisor panel.

Up to about one mile from the runway, beginning elevator and power adjustments should be made to achieve steady descent of approx. 1000 ft/min., aiming to touchdown about 500 ft. from beginning of the runway. As runway is approached, the thrust setting for the rate of sink should be kept steady and the aircraft allowed to keep sinking until a gradual check is made on sinking rate as the ground is approached with the elevator. At this time the attitude will increase and as the aircraft touches the ground the throttle should be gradually closed. Beware of closing the throttle too early as the aircraft will sink very rapidly and a heavy landing will result. If the speed is excessive

after crossing the runway - any elevator manipulation after touchdown may send the aircraft in the air again and heavy porpoise may result. In this case the stick should immobilized centrally and the aircraft allowed to damp the porpoise by itself. Any tendency to chase the aircraft motion will aggravate the situation. After touchdown the nose wheel should be put down gently on the runway — once firmly down, the parabrake should be streamed. It is extremely important that the location of the parabrake handle be checked several times before take off so there is no need for visual checking after landing. The parabrake is very effective but often erratic in behaviour and in the past has given severe swing tendency which must be instantaneously corrected with the brake. Maintain straight run until aircraft slows down using mainly brakes, as rudder effect is negligible with falling speed — there is no nose wheel steering. Jettison the parabrake on clearing the runway.

*"Spud" Potocki / Peter Cope ,
Malton 1958*

"Spud" Potocki climbs down from 205 after its one-and-only flight. Note that the main gear landing doors have been recycled to reduce buffeting against the fuselage while the gear is deployed... it improved lift as well. Flight tests look pretty routine; everybody just doing their job!

AVRO Photo

AVRO Photo

A funny incident happened just after "Spud" arrived in Malton. Jan Zurakowski recalls that "Spud" was responsible for a significant test pilot's pay raise. It seems that "Spud" wouldn't come to Canada because the salary offered was too low. No doubt, the two Poles connected instantly because of their common origins. While discussing their Gloster Test Pilot experiences, Jan learned that "Spud" was going to be earning 30% more than the other test pilots at Avro. Apparently an Avro test pilot's pay was not all that wonderful and a raise was badly needed. Well, as you may be surprised to learn, the pilots protested en mass and threatened to strike if the situation was not remedied. They got the increase !

Jan Zurakowski is smiling because "Spud" Potocki's employment was directly responsible for a much needed, and appreciated test pilot pay raise.

Elgin Scott

Peter Cope was a good friend of "Spud." They spent many weekends at Peter's cottage in the Muskokas. Do you notice... there wasn't much obesity in those days. What has happened to our food supply in the intervening years?

Swash-buckling Elgin Scott is a natural born Canadian. However, when you speak to him you immediately peg him as a member of the Polish community. He grew up in Poland. He escaped Poland during the Second World War and ended up in Britain flying in the Polish squadron with "Spud" Potocki and Jan Zurakowski. He told me many stories about "Spud." How did our friend get the name "Spud"? Apparently ground crews thought his nose looked like a potatoe. Elgin looks right at home in his P51 Mustang.

Elgin Scott

Elgin Scott

"Spud" Potocki at Peter Cope's cottage. Looking every bit the tuetonic warrior.

After cancellation, "Spud" Potocki stayed on at Avro for several years test flying the Avrocar, flying saucer. He next went to work for North American Aviation in Columbus, Ohio. A motel washroom repair accident blinded him in one eye and ended his flying career. (Is there justice in this world?) He died of Alzheimers disease in December of 1997. He will be remembered!

DND,DCIEM

F/L Doug Soper being
extracted from the cockpit
of the AVRO Arrow mock-
up during a heat stress
trial run early 1959. The
mock-up was situated at
the end of the production
line in bay #1.

Ian Higgins is climbing
into the Arrow wooden
mock-up, fully suited
up, to start crew
escapement trials. The
object was to test
reaction times and
whether or not the
escape sequence
should be linked so as
to get the pilots out as
fast as possible.

AVRO Photo

Human Factors Engineering

DND,DCIEM

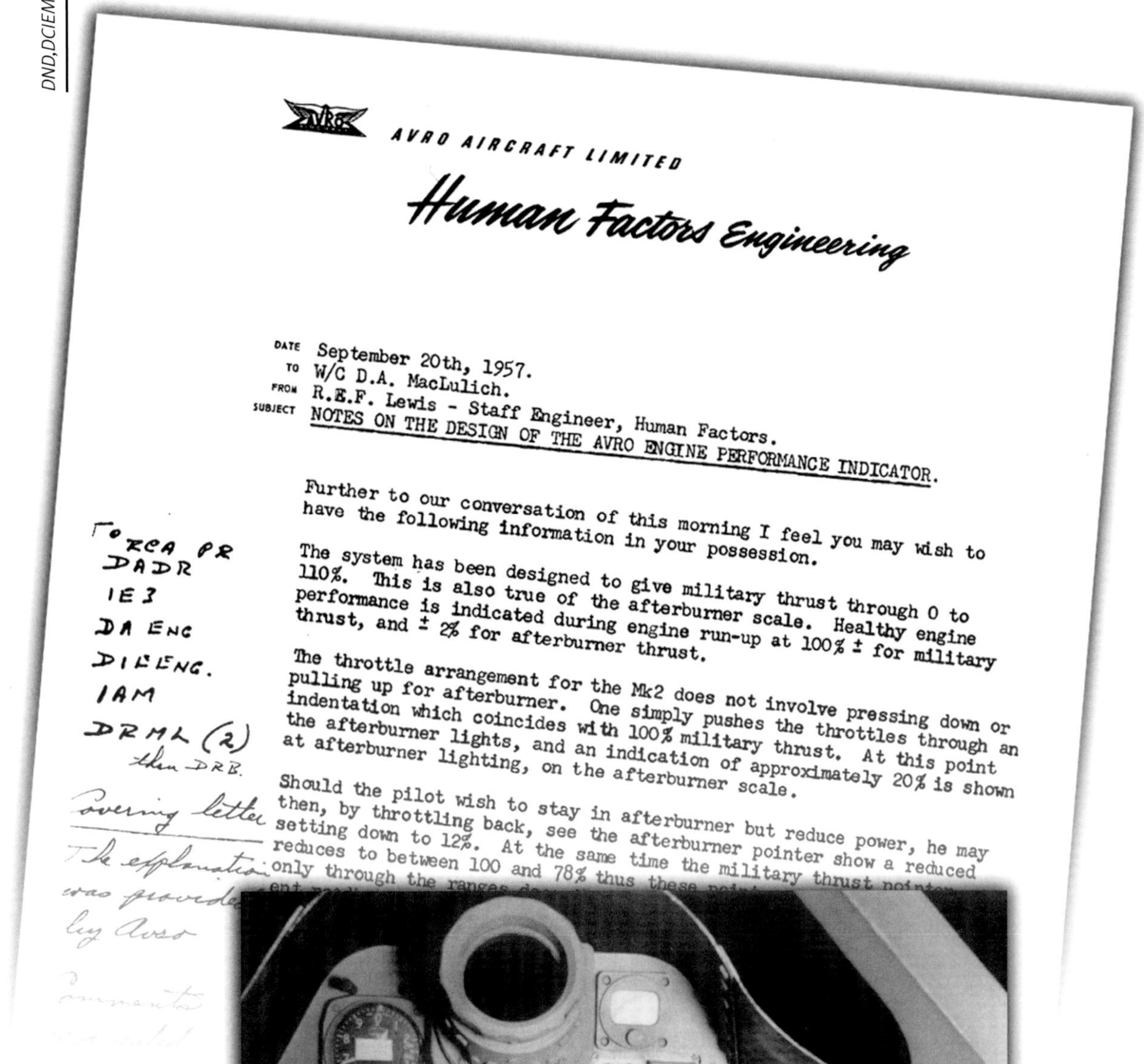

AVRO AIRCRAFT LIMITED

Human Factors Engineering

DATE September 20th, 1957.
TO W/C D.A. MacLulich.
FROM R.E.F. Lewis - Staff Engineer, Human Factors.
SUBJECT NOTES ON THE DESIGN OF THE AVRO ENGINE PERFORMANCE INDICATOR.

Further to our conversation of this morning I feel you may wish to have the following information in your possession.

The system has been designed to give military thrust through 0 to 110%. This is also true of the afterburner scale. Healthy engine performance is indicated during engine run-up at 100% ± for military thrust, and ± 2% for afterburner thrust.

The throttle arrangement for the Mk2 does not involve pressing down or pulling up for afterburner. One simply pushes the throttles through an indentation which coincides with 100% military thrust. At this point the afterburner lights, and an indication of approximately 20% is shown at afterburner lighting, on the afterburner scale.

Should the pilot wish to stay in afterburner but reduce power, he may then, by throttling back, see the afterburner pointer show a reduced setting down to 12%. At the same time the military thrust pointer reduces to between 100 and 78% thus these points ... only through the ranges ...

To ECA PR
DADR
IE3
DA Eng
DIE Eng.
IAM
DRML (2)
then DRB.

Covering letter
The explanation
was provided
by Avro

AVRO Photo

One of the first Arrow cockpit layouts. For pilots and Human Factors Engineers, this layout was nearly not useable. Visibility trials would bring old tried and true methods – such as the RAF blind flying panel display – back in vogue.

Ron Lewis was the principal Human Factors engineer at Avro, a new position created out of the rapid, and sometimes chaotic developments of World War II equipment. Man/machine efficiency was well thought out in the Arrow program. From the working cockpit to ground handling equipment new man/machine interfaces studies showed what gains could be had.

Special equipment is needed for Arrow aircrew to enable high altitude flying.

Ian Higgins, Avro Flight Test Department, tries on the first-base suit of the special flying kit which will protect the pilot after an "explosive decompression" and subsequent bail-out at 50,000 feet.

Human Factors engineering, as applied to the development of the Avro Arrow, really started coming into its own during the fifties. The need for and emphasis on getting it right really took hold. Ron Lewis, Human Factors engineer par excellence, was responsible for many of the advances made in this area. Close cooperation between DND's Institute of Aviation Medicine (DCIEM today) and Avro played a key role.

So what is Human Factors Engineering? Ron Lewis gave a lecture to the CAI in May of 1957 on the subject. Here is some of what he had to say.

"During the recent war, a great many new fighting machines were somewhat hurriedly developed. They – nearly all, no matter what their function – had controls: displays, work areas, and required men to operate them. The machines as such were reliable enough but men could often not operate them for a variety of reasons. For example, controls could not be reached, signals could not be heard or seen. Now you may wonder why the designers of this machinery did not adequately deal with these problems themselves? The fact is that they thought that they did, but detailed information about human performance was not available to the majority of engineers. Unfortunately, this meant that insufficient attention was given to the man/machine relationship and some true monstrosities were produced."

When dealing specifically with the aeronautical industry, Ron goes on to say;

"The problems confronting the human factors engineer in the aircraft industry are so varied the it is difficult to describe them within the scope of this talk…. The Human Factors Engineer, to be effective, must be involved at the design stage. Attempts to introduce this discipline later on in any programme will result only in compromise."

Ron goes on to illustrate, with examples, the problem of the Arrow, an aircraft crewed by a pilot and a navigator, and what other problems might arise. Here is some of the list he considered: the mission profile which sets the environmental conditions, information to be presented to the crew, design of the cockpit area, visibility, getting in and out, convenient placement of controls without being a contortionist, ejecting safely throughout the flight envelope, and more.

Let's have a look at some specifics, namely: the flight suit for high altitude flying and ejection, linking crew escape procedures, cockpit layout development and specifically the need for and placement of a side-slip (beta) indicator.

AVRO Photo

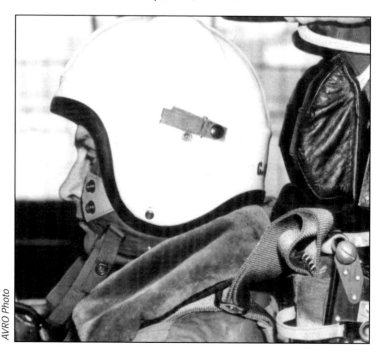

AVRO Photo

The Gentex H-4 helmet was standard issue for Arrow pilots. The inner helmet had radio earphones built right in to the fabric. The oxygen mask was clipped to the inner helmet. In fact, it was quite tight so that oxygen system pressure would not lift the mask from the face and break the seal. A sun-visor was optional.

Next is the pressure vest which maintains pressure on the chest making exhaling against oxygen mask back-pressure easier.

The Flight Suit:

The human body has a supply of water and food reserves but possesses no reserve supply of oxygen. A mere minute-and-a-half without it will severely damage the brain and could result in death. At sea level, we breath easily and oxygen transfers normally from the lungs to the blood stream. At ascending altitudes, the atmospheric pressure decreases and effects the bodies ability to absorb oxygen. To counter this, the cabin is pressurized with an oxygen supply, which increases to 100% above 34,000 feet. At this point, even sea level pressure is not sufficient to maintain the oxygen transfer, so it has to be forced into the lungs with greater pressure. Exhaling is increasingly more difficult against this back pressure. This can be offset if equal pressure is applied to the outside of the body. This could be done by pressurizing the cabin, but this could fail mechanically with the subsequent loss of pilot and aircraft.

The Arrow operational crew will wear a special suit and helmet to provide this pressure in a cabin that is only marginally pressurized. In the photos shown, Ian Higgins of Avro's flight test models the different pieces. The chest and head piece are for oxygen transfer, while the lower part of the body is pressurized seperately to keep blood in the upper part of the body when "G" is being pulled in a hard turn. (To turn the Arrow at mach 1.5, it takes a radius of 10 miles, pulling five gravities for about 5-10 minutes — quite the physical feat.)

The above combination can provide the pilot with enough oxygen exchange to survive a cabin pressure failure at 65,000 feet to be able to descend to lower levels where normal atmospheric breathing can resume. The selection and indoctrination of the pilot, and careful fitting of the equipment are essential features of this protection.

The observant reader will probably have noted that none of the pilots who actually flew the Arrow ever wore this outfit. They did use the standard oxygen mask, Gentex inner and outer helmet. In some of the pictures of "Spud" flying the Arrow, you can see he does use the upper pressure vest to control his breathing... but that was it, at least as far as flight test was concerned.

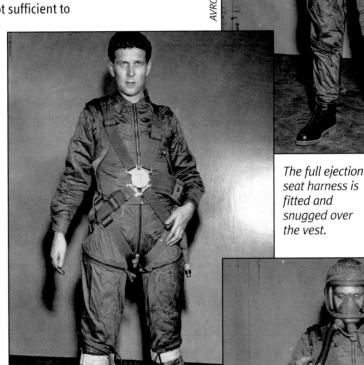

AVRO Photo

The full ejection seat harness is fitted and snugged over the vest.

AVRO Photo

Finally, the full face oxygen mask is put on. This full assembly was never used during the Arrow test program. It was being developed with the help of the Institute of Aviation Medicine.

AVRO Photo

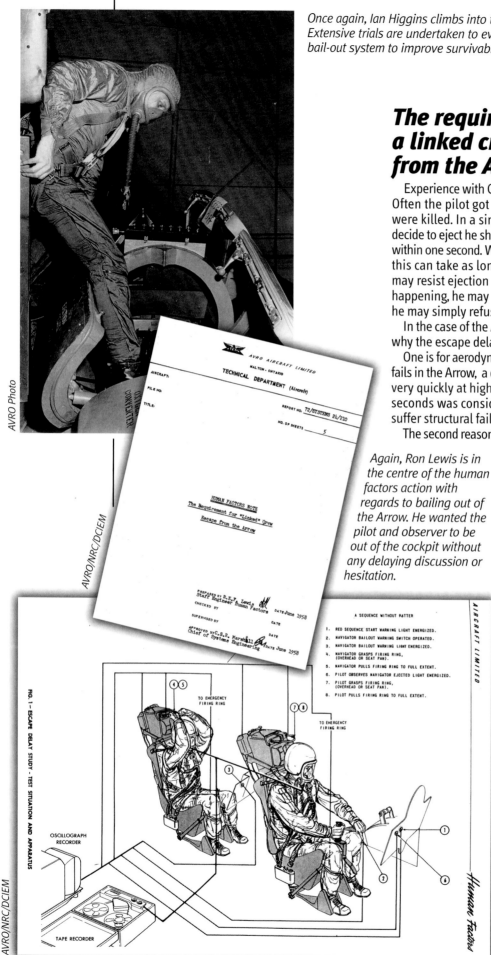

AVRO Photo

AVRO/NRC/DCIEM

Once again, Ian Higgins climbs into the Arrow wooden mock-up. Extensive trials are undertaken to evaluate the benefits of a "linked" bail-out system to improve survivability of the pilot /observer.

The requirement for a linked crew escape from the Arrow

Experience with CF-100 crew ejections were not great. Often the pilot got out without the navigator... many were killed. In a single seat airplane, should the pilot decide to eject he should be out and clear of the fuselage within one second. When two crew members are involved this can take as long as 13 seconds. The second party may resist ejection because he wants to know what is happening, he may not agree with the order to eject, or he may simply refuse to eject.

In the case of the Arrow, there were two clear reasons why the escape delay should be minimized.

One is for aerodynamic reasons. If the damping control fails in the Arrow, a diverging yaw condition can develop very quickly at high altitudes. Any delay beyond three seconds was considered too late – the aircraft would suffer structural failure.

The second reason is one of low altitude during takeoff and landing when power, structural, control, lack of fuel, to name a few conditions, would require ejection within a few seconds. This was amply demonstrated with several low level CF100 accidents.

Again, Ron Lewis is in the centre of the human factors action with regards to bailing out of the Arrow. He wanted the pilot and observer to be out of the cockpit without any delaying discussion or hesitation.

To overcome the hesitation to eject, it was proposed, for the Arrow programme, that a linked escape would:

1. Reduce total crew escape time to 2.5 seconds.
2. Permit the pilot, with one control, initiate escape, and to
3. Eliminate navigator hesitation or refusal.

When ejection was possibly needed, the pilot would make the decision... the observer followed. CF-100 bailouts were often fatal because crucial seconds were lost trying to evaluate if it was really necessary. Ron Lewis wanted to save flight crews!

AVRO Photo

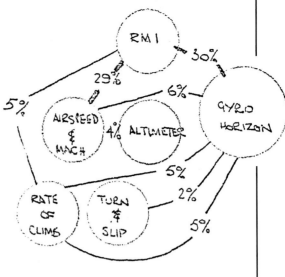

Early cockpit layouts proved to be unsatisfactory. Eye movement studies, and pilot familiarity with the more traditional placement and size of instruments spelled the end for this second to last configuration.

Layout of the Pilot's MKI Instrument Panel:

The instrument panel in the first layout had not been designed for flight test requirements. For example, the circular dial accelerometer is hard to read and has been replaced by the vertical Wynn version. The skin temperature gauge was virtually unused, and was diverted to the extreme right of the main instrument panel. Moving these instruments paves the way for other changes.

The sketches show eye movements during take-offs and landings. As might be expected, pilot's eye fixations are made through a narrow vertical band above and below the horizon. Frequently consulted instruments should therefore fall in an extension of that band, according to its priority. The proposed layout sketch and full double-page photograph clearly show how the eye fixations and six main instrument clusters fit into the eye movement bank. The front static boom probe has the alpha and

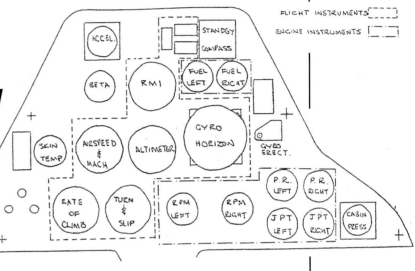

FLIGHT INSTRUMENTS
ENGINE INSTRUMENTS

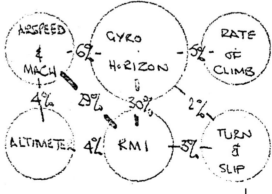

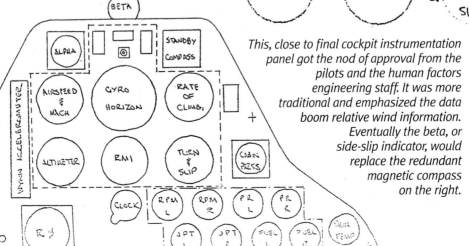

This, close to final cockpit instrumentation panel got the nod of approval from the pilots and the human factors engineering staff. It was more traditional and emphasized the data boom relative wind information. Eventually the beta, or side-slip indicator, would replace the redundant magnetic compass on the right.

AVRO/DCIEM

The final Arrow MkI cockpit mock-up. The very top instrument is the 'Beta Display,' showing the angle of sideslip. F/L Jack Woodman would use it to good effect during landing manouevres. The needle was centered with the heavy use of rudder. The small scope on the bottom left was never installed. Look at the Arrow Scrapbook for pictures of production Arrows cockpits. The view through the window places this mock-up on the second floor of the engineering department, facing north towards the experimental hangar which housed the wooden full-scale Arrow mock-up.

AVRO Photo

beta sensors built in. The angle of attack and sideslip motions indicated by this sensor are so important that they should be placed where eye movement is at a minimum.

Furthermore the placement of the "sacred" six instruments is a well tried and tested layout and has certain psychological advantages in their familiarity.

The final layout was only altered by placing the beta display on the main panel and dumping the magnetic stand-by compass. (See the actual MK I cockpit photo on the last page of this section.)

This approach reduced eye movements during the critical take-off and landing stages. Engine performance indicators could now be clustered at the bottom right of the panel and, spread out as in the earlier design.

The test pilots had a definite hand in evolving the cockpit layout. In fact, when Ron Lewis was finished, they heartily endorsed the improved safety of the new layout. When the Arrow leaves the ground, the skill of the pilot is at least enhanced by the ease with which instrument information is presented to him.

Ron Lewis, Avro's Human Factors Engineering guru, argues strongly for a prominently placed sideslip indicator for the Arrow. At low indicated air speeds, when directional stability is poor, incipient rolling may occur in the opposite direction of the casual sideslip. In the "gear down" mode especially, there is only limited automatic correction, so the pilot must be extra careful to eliminate sideslip as soon as it is detected.

AVRO *AIRCRAFT LIMITED*

MALTON — ONTARIO

TECHNICAL   DEPARTMENT   (Aircraft)

AIRCRAFT:

REPORT NO: 72/SYSTEM 12/230

FILE NO:

NO. OF SHEETS _____ 2

TITLE:

HUMAN FACTORS NOTE

THE REQUIREMENT FOR A 'BETA' DISPLAY

IN THE ARROW PILOTS COCKPIT

PREPARED BY R.E.F. Lewis _____ DATE July/58
Staff Engineer Human Factors

RECOMMENDED C.S.R. Marshall _____ DATE July/58
FOR APPROVAL Chief, Systems Engineering

APPROVED   F.H. Brame _____ DATE July/58
Chief of Technical Design

APPROVED   C.V. Lindow _____ DATE July/58
FOR RELEASE   Project Manager - Arrow

AVRO Report/DCIEM

The Requirement for a "Beta" Display in the Arrow Cockpit

There are occasions during Arrow flight when, in order to make appropriate control corrections, the pilot must know precisely the onset and extent of aircraft sideslip. The reader familiar with aerodynamics and instrumentation will remember that the ball in the turn and slip indicator does not indicate sideslip but only lateral acceleration sensed at the cockpit.

During landing in delta configured aircraft, if sideslip is not caught immediately a roll can be started in the opposite direction of the casual sideslip. Because the damper in the 'Gear Down Mode' has only limited automatic correction, the pilot must be very vigilant to detect this onset of sideslip. F/L Jack Woodman, in his flight notes, tells us of the amount of rudder work needed during the landing phase to keep the Arrow level. At high speed the Arrow was able to roll very quickly. If the pilot chose to fly the Arrow clean, i.e. without any artificial damping, beta instrument data was critically important.

Human factors engineering came into its own during the time of our Arrow. In later issues of this book, there will be more on this as we start to build the new Arrow.

AVRO Photo/Just before cut-up

Final MKI production cockpit. Note the two instruments at top on left and right side, alpha and beta indicators respectively.

You can see that the left side main undercarriage was completely sheared off. The side-stay is hanging on to the up jack on the outboard side of the wheel well. The telescoping side-stay is fully extended on the left side and broken away from the main gear. Substantial hydraulic and electrical damage is indicated.

AVRO Photo

RL201 has just left the west side of runway #32. The plane is still upright with the gear about to collapse all around. One can see that full right rudder has been applied by Jan Zurakowski throughout the landing roll but does not keep the plane on the runway. Jan thinks the side pull may be due to the chute not streaming properly... he decides to jettison it. It can be seen on the runway to the left of the aircraft.

AVRO Photo

Aerial view of RL201 accident scene. The plane was lifted by crane on to a flat bed carrier for the main fuselage. The front was supported independently and together they were hauled to the D-2 hangar for evaluation and repair.

AVRO Photo

RL201 Accident Investigation

Luckily no one was injured. The aircraft suffered, what appeared to be, very light damage for this type of accident.

REPORT ON ACCIDENT

TO

AVRO ARROW I 25201

ON

June 11, 1958

at

MALTON

UNCLASSIFIED

COMPILED BY:

P. Martin
Project Engineering - Arrow I

APPROVED BY:

F. F. Mitchell
Project Designer - Arrow I

170520

Official Avro Arrow RL201 accident investigation report found by the author in the National Research Council archives. It is by no means complete, although all the salient points of what happened that June 11/58 are there. It was superficial in its findings of a probable cause. Excellent photos of the damage are included.

AVRO Report/RCAF 1038N/NRC

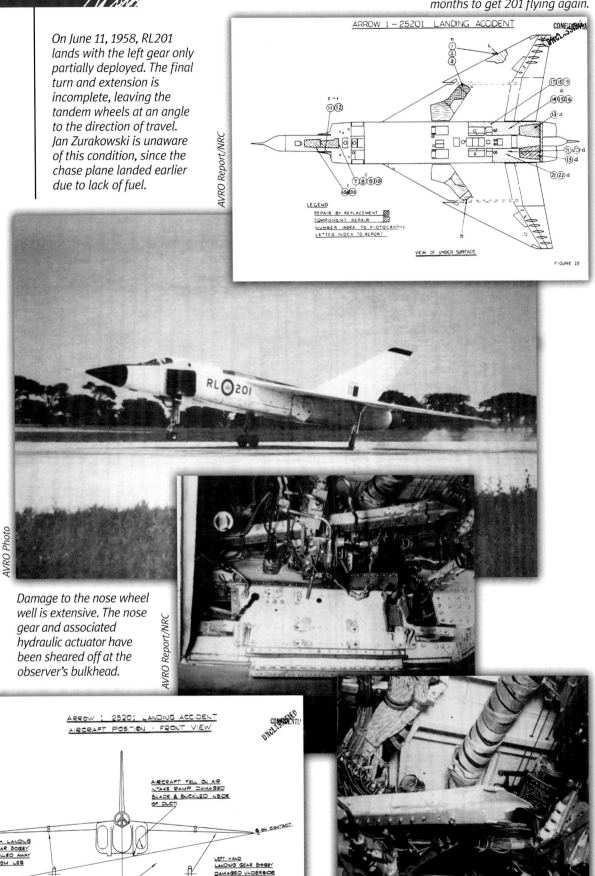

Overall plan view of the damage. It took nearly 4 months to get 201 flying again.

AVRO Report/NRC

ARROW 1 – 25201 LANDING ACCIDENT

LEGEND

REPAIR BY REPLACEMENT

COMPONENT REPAIR

NUMBER INDEX TO PHOTOGRAPHS

LETTER INDEX TO REPORT

VIEW OF UNDER SURFACE

FIGURE 25

On June 11, 1958, RL201 lands with the left gear only partially deployed. The final turn and extension is incomplete, leaving the tandem wheels at an angle to the direction of travel. Jan Zurakowski is unaware of this condition, since the chase plane landed earlier due to lack of fuel.

AVRO Photo

Damage to the nose wheel well is extensive. The nose gear and associated hydraulic actuator have been sheared off at the observer's bulkhead.

AVRO Report/NRC

ARROW 1 25201 LANDING ACCIDENT
AIRCRAFT POSITION · FRONT VIEW

AIRCRAFT FELL ON AIR
INTAKE RAMP DAMAGED
BLADE & BUCKLED INSIDE
OF DUCT

R.H. LANDING
GEAR BOGEY
PULLED AWAY
FROM LEG

LEFT HAND
LANDING GEAR BOGEY
DAMAGED UNDERSIDE
OF OUTER WING

NOSE LANDING GEAR
PULLED OUT OF
ATTACHMENTS,
ON NAVIGATORS
BULKHEAD & DAMAGED
NOSE WHEEL WELL

FIGURE 23

AVRO Report/NRC

AVRO Report/NRC

Some idea of the angle that RL201 came to rest at. Preliminary assessment showed damage to the left intake as well as the gear displacements.

Damage to RL201
Synopsis of RCAF report

Generally, the aircraft suffered very light damage for this type of accident.

The damage to the main gear pivot fittings and attachments appeared light; the nose wheel main attachment was completely torn away from the observer's bulkhead. The left hand air intake ramp was buckled badly. This area took most of the aircraft's weight on contact with the ground as the gear collapsed. The rear fuselage was badly buckled on the left side whereas the right side was light in comparison. When the skins were removed, the bulkheads were not as badly damaged as earlier thought and repair was relatively easy.

Radiographs and internal inspections showed no damage to the main supporting spars. The right gear pivots were OK. The left gear pivots needed reaming and bushing replacement. The outer wing did not require removal... only the dropped part was reskinned.

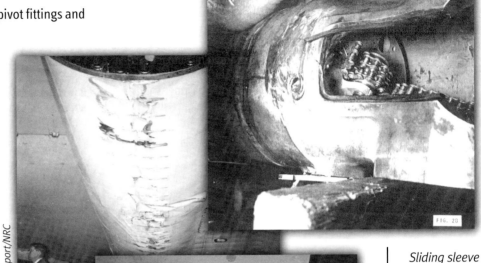

FIG. 20

AVRO Report/NRC

Sliding sleeve inside the ultra high strength steel outer casing of the main gear. It is this sleeve that did not fully extend and twist as the leg dropped by gravity and wind force. The anti-corrosion plating was either ground to close tolerance, or there was swelling of the cadmium plating layer due to hydrogen migration out of the casting. At any rate, it jammed.

ENGINE ACCESS

ENGINE ACCESS

AVRO Report/NRC

Damage to the underside of RL201 is lighter than the undercarriage areas. Although extensive, skin removal and bulkhead repairs where quickly completed. The engine access panels look more damaged than they were, and still functioned. The duct bay lower air ejector was filled with dirt but basically still functional. The hydraulic access panel is seen in the top left portion of the bottom photo.

37

Likely cause of incomplete main gear extension

A chain assembly pulls the inner shaft of the main gear up and, while shortening the overall leg, rotates it through some 36 degrees. On deploying the gear, drag and gravity forces reversed this sequence. Early on in the program, Avro felt a chain dust cover was needed at the top end of the gear to ensure that nothing got into the inner shaft area which might block its decent. Apparently, Dowty did not agree but carried out the required modification. Because of this change, early accident investigation was centered on this modification as a probable cause. More in-depth work revealed that this particular gear was sluggish in its operation right from the start. Tracing its manufacture through its various steps, it was discovered that, rust inhibiting cadmium plating of the ultra high tensile steel inner shaft varied in thickness and was properly ground to be within tolerance.

During the plating operation, hydrogen migrates into the steel and slowly bakes its way out. With the cadmium plating in place the hydrogen on leaving the steel swelled the cadmium changing its thickness... in RL201's case so much that the gear stuck.

It was feared that the left main gear, after being stressed during the landing and finally collapsing and ripping out of its sockets, had damaged the main spar and pivot joint at the leading edge of the wing. Extensive inspection, including x-rays, found the main spar to be intact. The forward pivot hole, however, was twisted and could not accept a new gear. A special reaming tool was made, as shown in this photo, that over-sized a new hole in which a correct sized bushing was fitted.

AVRO /NRC

A broader view of the left underside of RL201, looking outward, shows the area of repair undertaken. Note the repair work on the outer wing extension and droop. The triangular piece, at the transport joint of the inner and outer wings, provides additional strength and is usually covered with a fairing.

The right gear also collapsed, but was easily replaced, as shown in this repaired view. The left side of the aircraft took most of the hit and damage.

The solution

Plating was needed for rust protection. Hydrogen migration with plating is a fact of life. How do you get rid of the hydrogen, or at least keep it in place? The normal routine is to bake the metal at high temperature so that it bubbles out. This is not possible with the gear because the much needed heat treat would be lost. The solution was to coat the steel with a flash plating of inert gold and then plate over it with the cadmium. The gold stopped the hydrogen from getting out.

A molecular physics solution to reliable main gear operation!

AVRO /NRC

The slap on the wrist

As would be heard many more times, the RCAF felt that better communication between Dowty and Avro would have revealed earlier that, due to such close fits, binding of these mating parts would become a source of trouble!

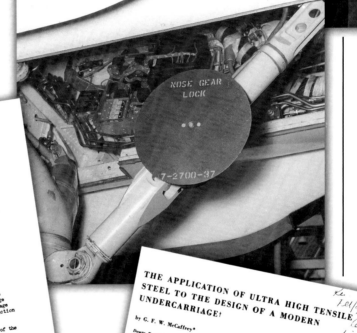

The repaired nose wheel gear is in place. The locking strut and ground safety pin are central. The black transformer above the safety pin regulates the de-icer circuits on the air intakes.

RCAF 1038CN/National Archives

A visit to Dowty's Ajax plant convinced the RCAF TSD unit personnel that the accident was manufacturing tolerances related. They conclude that better communication between Avro and Dowty might have prevented this particular gear from being used.

CAI journal explains the building and metallurgy of the Arrow main gear in detail.

CAI Journal

Orenda Iroquois
Jewel of the Arrow program

Orenda Photo, Family

Orenda Photo, Family

Earle Brownridge started at Avro Canada in the forties as a time keeper. As the company grew and split into Avro Aircraft and Orenda Engines, Earle's abilities and dedication were recognized and he became Works Manager. At cancellation, he was Executive Vice President and General Manager of all of Orenda. Today, this progress would not happen without a lot of formal education... too bad!

Charles Grinyer, Orenda's Vice President Engineering, unassuming, tireless, and exacting giant, guided the Iroquois development from its birth to its demise. He said, "It was a nasty business from the beginning!" I was as surprised by this statement as, no doubt, you are!

ORENDA ENGINES LIMITED
MALTON — CANADA

OFFICE OF THE
EXECUTIVE VICE PRESIDENT
AND GENERAL MANAGER

December 16, 1958

PERSONAL

Dear Charles:

The end of 1958 is drawing near and I therefore
feel it is an appropriate time to make a few comments
on some of the happenings of the past year.

First of all I want to thank you very much indeed
for accepting me as your General Manager last March
and doing this in a manner that gave great confidence
to my boss that Orenda was in fairly good hands.

Since that time your complete loyalty and devotion
in trying to make this company a success deserves the
highest praise. As you know we have not solved all of
the problems with regard to the future of Orenda, but
with people like yourself behind me I have no fears for
the future.

Thanks very much for all you are doing and have
done.

Best wishes and a prayer for a more enjoyable 1959.

Sincerely,

Earl.

Mr. C. A. Grinyer,
Vice-President - Engineering

June Chubb, Grinyer Family

Both Earle and Charles respected each other's talents as this letter bears out. Charles Grinyer had tendered his resignation after he found out that the French had backed out of a possible major order because of rumours that the Canadian Government was going to cancel the program. O'Hurley, the then Minister of the Department of Defence Production, called Grinyer, personally and assured him it was not so. (As bold a lie as any, as later Cabinet documents would unfold!) Grinyer agreed to stay only to be disappointed a short few months later.

The Iroquois MKII, X116, ready to be taken over to Avro Aircraft for fitting in RL206. The fastest jet engine power plant in the world is ironically parked beside a 'go slow' sign.

Orenda Photo

"It was a nasty business from the beginning,"
Charles Grinyer's view of the Iroquois development program...

Orenda Photo

The Orenda was the fore-runner of the Iroquois. According to Grinyer it was a great commercial success but from a technical point of view he called it 'copy-cat engineering.' It worked and was used principally to power the CF-100 and Canadian built Sabre jets. Some 4,000 would eventually be built. Sir Roy Dobson is congratulating representatives of the production team while a beaming Earle Brownridge looks on.

About one year after the Arrow Scrapbook was published, I received a phone call from June Chubb, Charles Grinyer's daughter, from Caledon, ON. She had just received my book and asked the bookstore, in nearby Orangeville, for my number. She explained that her father wished to speak to me about the Iroquois engine, and would I come for a visit. She further told me that Charles was a bit of a recluse and had refused numerous requests for interviews over many years. I was delighted, honoured, and accepted of course.

Charles looked pretty good for a man in his late nineties, albeit frail.

We introduced each other and talked tid-bits as one does while getting comfortable with one another.

"Your book has caused me many a sleepless night," he said.

"How so?" I replied.

Orenda Photo

In 1953, the Hawker Siddeley Group Design Council journeyed to North America to attend celebrations of the 100th anniversary of powered flight... remembering Kitty Hawk. The Group's Canadian holdings were now extensive and detailed visits were organized. Here the Group's executives and technical chiefs meet in the Orenda lunch room. Can you pick them out? Dobson, Sprigg, Smye, Gordon, Brownridge, McLachlan, Smith and of course Grinyer.

Here's the story.

In the Arrow Scrapbook, I indicated that we had uncovered three Iroquois engines, the experimental one from the B47, X104 which had been at the National Research Council for icing trials, and X116, which was loaned to Bristol Siddeley after cancellation and now in storage at the Hendon, RAF museum in the UK. From these three engines, we might try to get one running, at least in a kind of curious way. Charles said that just before cancellation, the seventh stage compressor rotor was throwing blades without any conclusive solution determined. He was worried that we would try an engine and basically, get into trouble by trying to run it too fast. He suggested to by all means try it, but keep the rpm below 90%, as a safety limit. He said it was an amazing thing: a rotor can be perfect, a blade can pass all inspection, but put them together as a unit and they fail! He

suspected that aerodynamic forces were at play, setting up vibrations that would only show up in an assembled unit. Another potential source of problem was the blade manufacture itself -— some basic defect in the forgings. Today, blades are grown from a single crystal, hence more pure and strong as well as exhibiting predictable properties. At any rate, his concern was cautionary yet encouraging.

Later on, he said some amazing things about the Iroquois Programme.

The notion that the whole programme was a nasty business right from the start is most curious. Charles explained that when the RCAF got involved the government wanted in on all the technology as it developed. The company, on the other hand, wanted to maintain some sense of propriety and special expertise that would not be shared around

43

Hawker Siddeley executives view the running of an Orenda in the Plant #2 test cells on the south-east side of the building. Interestingly enough, Jim Floyd, Avro's chief engineer, is present to see the evolving power plant for his later baby, the Avro Arrow. The test cell was state of the art for its day. It still exists today.

the industry. This was especially true of work on special alloys and handling techniques. Charles told me how he would acquire contracts with Atomic Energy of Canada Ltd., which were really research projects for the Iroquois, so that he would not be obliged to divulge the results to the Department of Defence Production. He talked about the use of titanium, how scarce it was at the time and how promising it would be for the programme. It wasn't just the specific gravity difference that was a 40% weight-saving over steel, but because of the lighter

blades. For example, the spindle holding the blades could also be lighter due to lower blade loading. Real weight savings of assembled parts might be in the order of 70%. Amazing!

Another issue involved the capacity of Orenda to actually produce good research that would lead to the new engine technology. He told me that the Orenda engine was really copy-cat engineering, and that nothing revolutionary was involved. It was a direct scaling of the Chinook and operated in a known regime. A commercial success but no engineering marvel. When he arrived in Canada (and Avro Canada Ltd. in 1953) he set out to build a basic research capacity that would make the skipping of a generation of engine possible.

The new engine would have about 20% of its development in completely unknown areas, i.e. "beyond the state of the art." He wanted to do it from the ground up. The most challenging thing was to stay within the weight limitation that the new Arrow would impose, 4500 lbs. and a thrust of 24,000 lbs. The two-spool arrangement was lighter than a single compressor, aside from it being more flexible in performance. Material research in basic properties, handling, machining and welding were the order of the day. The use of the scarce titanium showed that there were problems as well. It was found out that titanium was a poor conductor of heat. If it was used in the stator blades, a developing rub could build up

heat and ignite the titanium, it burns like magnesium. Furthermore excessive hydrogen dissolved in the titanium could lead to a weakened blade. Successfully baking the metal in a vacuum to 'bubble it out' became a standard operating procedure, but not before it nearly caused the cancellation of its use.

Because high required thrust was coupled to high turbine/exhaust temperatures, it was thought from the beginning, that some form of turbine blade cooling would be needed. Considerable work was undertaken to manufacture hollow blades which would receive air from the compressor, pass through the structure, and keep it cool. Work by Inco was progressing on a new alloy that would take the higher temperature. It required casting a blade instead of the forging, which was the established way. The decision was taken to abandon the cooling option in favour of the new Inco casting alloy, which retained efficiency and also a simpler design.

Peter Zuuring Photo

The same test cell today, still in use at Magellan Aerospace, Orenda's new corporate owner. It is the only one left with the fifties equipped instrumentation. When it is scrapped, it should be retained lock, stock, and barrel for an interesting museum exhibit. The facilities built during the Arrow period were first class. As in Avro, they saw active service for decades. Too bad we destroyed the newer test cells and the High Altitude Test Facility so that we could have a bingo hall at the Malton International Convention Centre.

Orenda Photo

Looking to the south-west, we can see the original Plant #1 and smaller Sopwith Lab attached to its North side. The Iroquois was built there. Grinyer's systematic testing of materials under operating conditions in the lab led to many of the innovations that made the Iroquois possible. Today, Torontonians will recognize the building cluster as being part of the International Centre, few people know of the intense work and accomplishments that were experienced there.

Similar engineering efforts were pioneered with respect to the after-burning section of the engine. A four-stepped approach was abandoned in favour of fully variable, integrated, design which allowed for completely throttleable thrust while in re-heat -– a breakthrough.

When you sit with a person of the calibre of Charles Grinyer, you feel humbled pretty quickly. He was especially recognized by his staff and management. They worked hard for him. He got results. The Iroquois was tested at the USAF Arnold Engineering Development Centre in Tennesee. I had the opportunity to talk to the Director of the new Museum down there. He dug around for me, and found out that quite a bit of information is still available from the fall of 1958 and early 1959. Tests were in full swing when cancellation came. It was a surprise to everyone involved. Because of the suddenness of the action worked was stopped immediately with many half-finished reports just languishing around. Eventually they were gathered up and just put into dead library storage. Well, they have been recovered and will come back to Canada. Some of the people that worked on the project are still alive and were asked by the director,

"Well, what did you think?"

The reply,

"The Iroquois was quite something, amazing engineering...we didn't see the like of it for another 10 years!"

After cancellation, the RCAF knew that the Iroquois programme had many ground-breaking firsts and was considered by many to be the leader of the day. Instead of keeping it going, they thought it would be worthwhile to document the actual engineering advances achieved in developing the Iroquois. Nice of them, wasn't it?

The Termination Reports, covering these state-of-the-art advances, were prepared through the office of the Chief of the Air Staff, by Wing Commander H.K. Hollingsworth and coordinated by C.E. Elliot, Contract and Parts Manager at Orenda. About five man-months of work and $60,000 later, the reports are classified into four sections, Materials, Mechanical Design, Performance and Manufacturing Techniques. What follows is a summary.

Orenda Photo

1. *Materials:*

The Iroquois programme led to considerable advances in the use of titanium and knowledge and methods of working the material including welding. This knowledge led to breakthroughs in handling other materials such as zirconium, of interest to the nuclear industry.

A variety of new alloys and complex applications were encountered which required improved fabrication and welding techniques. Development work was done on processes and procedures, such as the effect of stress relieving high temperature metals/materials by shot peening through quantitative creep and fatigue testing.

The work done on plastic compressor blades with fiberglass and asbestos reinforcement represented a considerable advance with applications to both aeronautical, and commercial machinery. This would result in extended life and reliability combined with significant reduction in weight and cost.

Work on turbine blade cooling involved investigation of forged and cast materials suitable for hollow structures.

The fully air-conditioned new Plant #2 was built for the Orenda production line. It was of modular design for easy and rapid expansion, should the cold war demand it. Air temperature was controlled so that machining tolerances were uniform and parts that were designed for hot operation could be machined at room-temperature with predictable operating temperature dimensions. It included Orenda's administrative, engineering, and sales offices. It still stands today, with 1/10th of the work force. Orendas are still being serviced for pipe-line and electrical generating service.

Orenda Photo

Group executives are once again getting a gentleman's tour of the new Plant #2 facility. Detailed models were built to study plant material flow and work efficiency. They were useful in that they also provided visitors with a bird's-eye-view of the whole operation before going down into the plant itself. Recognize anybody?

47

Orenda Photo

Orenda Engines' extensive engineering/design office. As was the case with Avro, these large open work spaces allowed easy communication. No computers, no phones but lots of paper and slide rules. With, what would be called, primitive tools today, they designed the most advanced jet engine in the world. The Iroquois skipped a generation in concept, and was flexible enough to grow with variants to cover many different applications.

2. Mechanical Design:

The structural design of the Iroquois, providing a thrust to weight ratio of over five, yet retaining a high degree of structural reliability, ruggedness, and simplicity, was a considerable state-of-the-art advance.

The oil lubricating system of the Iroquois was completely novel, incorporating a wholly internal air venting system requiring no overboard connections, and ensuring adequate internal pressure to prevent circulating pump cavitation at low ambient pressure conditions, i.e. high altitudes.

Root fixing methods and design aspects of plastic blades was new.

The design of compressor blade attrition seals and the mechanical aspects of shrouded stators and labyrinth seals was advanced. Right after cancellation other engine manufacturers wanted this information.

Industrial turbines were made more competitive through work done on turbine blade cooling. Heat transfer and fabrication problems were solved. The various configurations, investigations and reasons for final choices and relatively simple design could be of great interest.

At a fairly late stage in the development of the Iroquois, a completely new problem was encountered, that of aerodynamic stimulation of compressor/turbine blade vibration. Work on this problem will be of interest to others in the field. (Author's note: Recall that Grinyer told me that 7th stage compressor blades were failing towards the end of the programme... the problem of operational stimulation of vibrational forces leading to blade failure was what he was worried about.)

It is impossible to guarantee that a compressor will never throw a blade. At Orenda, during the course of the Iroquois programme, methods and design of ballistic protection for surrounding structures was advanced.

Blade root fixture failure received intensive investigation. Results of work done to alleviate this problem involved, for example, fret welding, shot peening and lubrication will be of interest.

It was found that textbook approaches to operations at critical speeds fell far short of reality. For example bearing flexibility at high speeds was investigated and new solutions found.

The operating experience and design methodology of the rear, high temperature, end of the Iroquois will be of interest to those concerned with dimensional stability and structures operating in this regime.

The self-squaring after-burner nozzle was a breakthrough, and has potential interest because of its contribution to hydraulic system simplification.

Orenda Photo

The first Iroquois MKI mock-up on display in 1954. The design team came up with the basic layout in just twenty days. The project was labeled PS-13 (Project Study 13.) It was a project initiated by Orenda, approved unanimously by the Group's design council, yet not funded by the RCAF until two years later.

48

3. Performance:

Considerable knowledge was gained in estimating two-shaft engine performance and the relationship between turbine/compressor characteristics in order to achieve the required performance.

Advances in predicting surges, the nature of rotational stalls and its elimination by variable inlet guide vanes was new.

The Iroquois was the first to successfully run a transonic compressor and represented a major advance in aerodynamics.

The use and merits of hydro-mechanical and electronic controls was considerably advanced.

The Iroquois combustion chamber operated at higher operating velocities than was generally practiced at the time. The oxygen relight and enrichment system was novel. After cancellation, many were interested in this development.

Reduction of noise was investigated and findings would be of interest to any manufacturer contemplating the use of jet engines in the public domain.

The development of special instrumentation was advanced. High speed slip rings, temperature, pressure and vibration probes were used throughout the engine to obtain experimental information. The data logging methods/ hardware used in the test cells and in the B47 test programme would have many other industrial applications.

4. Manufacturing Techniques:

The design and development of advanced tooling, fabrication and assembly techniques parallels the design of the engine itself.

Sheet metal fabricating techniques in general and in particular as applied to metal blades will be of interest to many. Considerable effort went into brazing techniques.

The manufacture and quality control of reinforced plastic blades was new.

The fabricating techniques and processes of hollow turbine blades will be of interest.

In general, quality control of system manufacturing and assembly were developed and optimized.

The Iroquois development was the jewel of the Arrow programme!

The vertical build of the Iroquois in plant #1 is underway. This first prototype came together in less than a year.

Orenda Photo

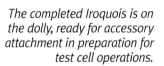

The completed Iroquois is on the dolly, ready for accessory attachment in preparation for test cell operations.

Orenda Photo

The instrumented Iroquois is now ready on the test stand. First running of the engine was in Dec/54. Within one year significant performance milestones were achieved with sustained operation in excess of of 20,000 lbs of thrust at maximum speed.

Orenda Photo

AVRO Photo

Iroquois MKII mock-up including Arrow insertion
trolley. This display was presented to the
Engineering Development Conference for the
Avro Arrow MKII held at Avro's Malton facility in
September/57.

Orenda Photo

First 'Official' photo of the
Iroquois released to the
public. There is a lot more
room in the newly
commissioned test cells
just west of Plant #2.

Official roll-out of the Iroquois was on Monday, July 22, 1957. A much
smaller affair than the Arrow's roll-out in October of the same year, it
was none-the-less, a well attended occasion. Orenda executives hosted
defence, political, supplier, foreign and employee dignitaries.

"The Orenda," July 26, 1957

Orenda Photo

A clear view looking west. The test cells are nearly completed. The High Altitude Test facility is under construction. The building in the background is Plant #1 and to the right the Sopwith Lab. On the horizon you can just make out Avro's experimental hangar. Once the cells are in use the stacks are blackened by the hot engine exhaust.

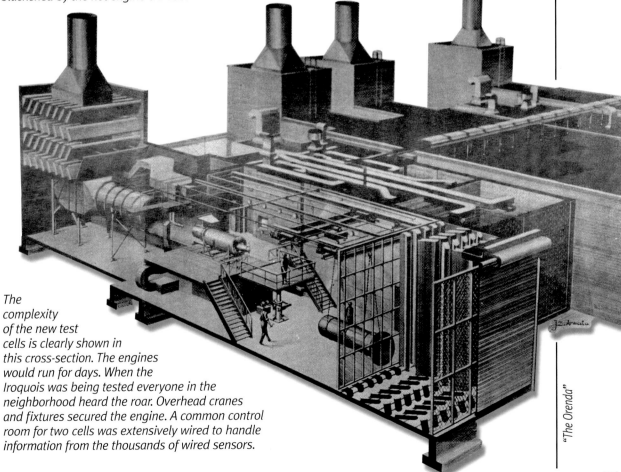

The complexity of the new test cells is clearly shown in this cross-section. The engines would run for days. When the Iroquois was being tested everyone in the neighborhood heard the roar. Overhead cranes and fixtures secured the engine. A common control room for two cells was extensively wired to handle information from the thousands of wired sensors.

"The Orenda"

51

AVRO Photo

Herb Saravanemuto, bottom right, gave me these photos of Orenda engineers getting an evening briefing on the Arrow by Robert Lindley. Lots of interest and obvious enthusiasm.

The Orenda engineers were split up into small groups and given an extensive tour of Avro's production facility. Herb can be seen once again looking into RL206's cockpit and navigator positions. It stood at the end of the bay #1 production line. The oxygen system is clearly visible behind the navigator's bulkhead.

AVRO Photo

AVRO Photo

Iroquois X-116 has just been delivered to Avro. Its twin, X-115, threw a blade on the seventh stage compressor and was getting re-tested. It never made it! X-116 was transferred to Avro's dolly and test fitted in RL-206. It was to be used for taxi trials only. X-117/8 were to be the first Iroquois to fly in the Arrow.

Orenda/Chubb Family

A. V. ROE CANADA LIMITED

May 19, 1959.
Dict. May 15.

Dear Charles:

This is to acknowledge your letter of today, in which you tender your resignation as a Director of Orenda, which I accept but with deep feeling and regret.

Under the circumstances I feel that you have made the correct decision. However, in my view it is a national calamity that circumstances should exist as they do.

I wish to take this opportunity of extending to you my deep personal gratitude for the great contribution which you made, not only to the company, but to the industry as a whole. In my official capacity, I also wish to extend the same sentiments on behalf of the Directors of Orenda Engines Limited, and A. V. Roe Canada Limited. You know, I am sure, that you take with you our very best wishes for your continued success, and for the well-being of yourself and your family.

Sincerely yours,
FRED T. SMYE.

Mr. C. A. Grinyer,
C/o Orenda Engines Limited,
Malton, Ont.

A.V. Roe Canada Limited/Chubb Family

Fred Smye accepts Charles Grinyer's resignation as a Director of Orenda Engines Limited. The content speaks for itself. Stock options significantly boosted an executive's pay, until cancellation that is!

ORENDA ENGINES LIMITED
MALTON — CANADA

Mr. C. A. Grinyer,
V/P Engineering.

3rd June, 1959.

Dear Charles:

On accepting your resignation as an officer and director of Orenda Engines Limited and Orenda Industrial Limited I find it very difficult to adequately put into words my feelings of gratitude for your great contribution to these companies.

I believe you know Charles that I have the greatest respect for you personally and for your abilities. Your enthusiasm, integrity, loyalty and knowledge are, in my opinion, unequalled, and your ideals of living, your home life and close ties with your family are well respected.

I regret very much, as you well know, that the situation here at Orenda at the present time is such that the type of work we will be doing in the future would not be to your liking. Therefore, your decision to accept the position of Vice-President, Engineering of Atomic Energy of Canada was a wise one and I repeat that I do not know of anyone in this country better qualified to fill this position.

Orenda will be looking forward to working closely with Atomic Energy on future projects and in this way we hope that we will be seeing a good deal of you and therefore perhaps feel that we have not lost you completely.

My very best wishes go with you and your wife for continued good health and happiness in your new surroundings.

Yours sincerely,

E.K.Brownridge
EM

Earle Brownridge accepts Grinyer's resignation as V.P. of Engineering. Again the content speaks for itself although it is a much more personal letter. Brownridge was a leader of men! He didn't stay much longer, and went on to found American Motors of Canada, a substantial enterprise north-east of Brampton.

Chubb Family

Peter Zuuring

On leaving, Charles Grinyer was presented with a small scale model of the Iroquois. I haven't seen another like it. It represents the MKI as indicated by the shape of the after-burner. Charles told me that if they had only had one more year on the project, the Iroquois would truly have met its revolutionary goals. Instead, he sadly reflected, "I wasted seven years of my life!" The rest of his career was spent with Atomic Energy of Canada, first as Chief Engineer, then as V.P. of Engineering.

Charles Albert Grinyer was born in England March 8, 1903. His stubborn father refused him a formal education to prevent putting on airs. A Gas Works apprenticeship placed him in a position were his quick thinking saved a substantial part of the works during a major fire. The owners were so pleased that they provided the time and means for Charles to obtain his engineering training. The war years found Charles in the War Ministry, helping to develop aircraft engines. During this time he was in contact with the father of the jet engine Sir Frank Whittle. Bristol aircraft was his next stop en route to his greatest achievement at Orenda engines... the mighty Iroquois. Walter Mclachlan, Orenda's President and General Manager had the following to say about Charles at the official unveiling of the engine, "There is one member of the Orenda team who merits special mention today. This man has organized and led this project in a completely devoted spirit. His initiative, courage, and technical foresight have been an inspiration to all of us who have been associated with the Iroquois programme. I refer to Charles Grinyer our Vice-president of Engineering at Orenda." After the Arrow programme cancellation, Charles left Orenda a disillusioned man. He finished his working career at Atomic Energy of Canada, first as Chief Engineer and then Vice-president of Engineering. This unassuming giant of a man died in Orangeville during March 2001. He was much respected and loved by his family. He will not be forgotten!

Sir Roy Dobson, Crawford Gordon and the Arrow...caught by the camera in a prophetic stance. The Father, Son and Holy Ghost – casualties in the big stakes game of continental defence, government ineptitude and corporate arrogance.

AVRO Photo

Father, Son and Holy Ghost

More Vignettes and Curiosities

A continuation of the popular section pioneered in the Arrow Scrapbook...

RCAF, 1038CN, National Archives

RCAF
SIGNALS OFFICE

JUL 23   03 29 '59

```
NNNNEFA080MA079
MM RFEPGJ RFEPFZ
DE RFEPMR 411/22
M 221959Z
FM CANAIRMAT
TO RFEPGJ/1202 TSD MALTON
INFO RFEPGJ/12TSU WESTON
RFEPFZ/CANAIRHED
BT
QTO447 22 JUL
AFHQ 1038CN-80 DMS 8 JUL PD FIVE ARROW AIRFRAMES 25201 25202 25203
25204 AND 25205 ARE ALLOTTED FROM AVROE CONTRACT REPAIR IN
ACCORDANCE WITH CAP 16 VOL 12.13 TO STRIKE OFF HAVING BEEN
TURNED OVER TO DDP FOR DISPOSAL ACTION ON AUTHORITY OF DND LETTER
1038CN-80 AMTS 27 APR TO DDP PD AIRFRAMES ARE TO BE STRUCK OFF
CHARGE BY CERTIFICATE ISSUE VOUCHER PD THE CIV IS TO MAKE REFERENCE
TO THE ABOVE NOTED LETTER AND IS TO BE CROSS REFERRED TO THE ORIGINAL
RECEIPT VOUCHER THAT BROUGHT AIRFRAMES TO RCAF ACCOUNTABILITY
PD QTO ON ENGINES WILL BE ISSUE AT A LATER DATE
BT
22/1959Z
```

The RCAF communicates to the Technical Service Detachment at Avro that the five airframes are to be taken off the roll and handed over to the Department of Defence Production for disposal. Note the date. By this time, they have already been torched!

Furthermore, by this time, Crawford Gordon has also been torched and is about to resign! Was someone just covering their hind quarters? I think we were all casualties!

So much fascinating stuff continues to come to light, that it is hard to choose some highlights for this first issue of *Arrow Countdown*. For the most part, I have stayed with the two page spread that makes it easy to pick up and put down. Get ready for some surprises!

Jetliner
1949 - 1959

It is amazing that one of the projects resurrected after the Arrow's cancellation is the old Jetliner. The new incarnation looks like a DC-8 knock-off. It still sports the regional jet configuration of about 40 passengers. It is surprising that AVRO would choose such a project, since the big US players such as Boeing and McDonnell etc. are in the market with inter-continental products themselves. The valid idea of a Canadian regional jet would take some 30 more years to come to fruition.

AVRO Publishing

Brochures of the two regional jets – one innovative and the other a rehash.

Reporters line up to get an inside view of Avro's new Jetliner... on the tarmac at Malton in August of 1949. Avro sure had cutting edge ideas yet was frustrated by circumstance and inept governments much to Canada's misfortune.

A.V. Roe Canada Limited

Looks like a miniature DC-8 to me! Falling back on rejected projects has never worked for anyone.

AVRO Publishing

The flight envelope mirrored the original Jetliner. Was this suggestion a make work project in a desperate attempt to salvage something of the great enterprise which, only weeks before, had so much promise?

AVRO Publishing

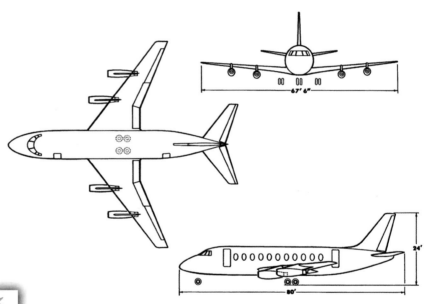

AVRO AIRCRAFT LIMITED

3-VIEW GENERAL ARRANGEMENT

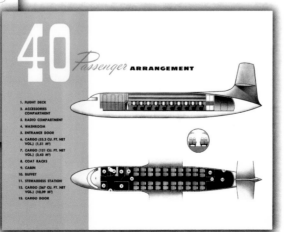

AVRO AIRCRAFT LIMITED

SEATING ARRANGEMENT (44 PASSENGERS)

The new brochure had less gloss, yet was clearly modeled on the original publication of the 1949 Jetliner.

AVRO Publishing

When you look, stuff just keeps surfacing! This thick Avrocar programme report was found in the NRC's, CISTI rare book room library.

Avrocar...
More about Avro's secret VTOL projects.

J69 motor being delivered to Avro from Orenda testing facilities for installation in the Avrocar. It was delivered at the same time as the Iroquois II, X-116 for test fitting in Arrow RL-206 and ground running. Two advanced projects that, in the end, did not see the light of day.

The Avro car, looking pretty sleek, is rolled out of the shop – no fanfare – located at the south-west corner of Avro's # 3 Bay.

All Avro's documentation was superb. It had a consistent style, clear content and a pleasure to browse. This cutaway is just one more example.

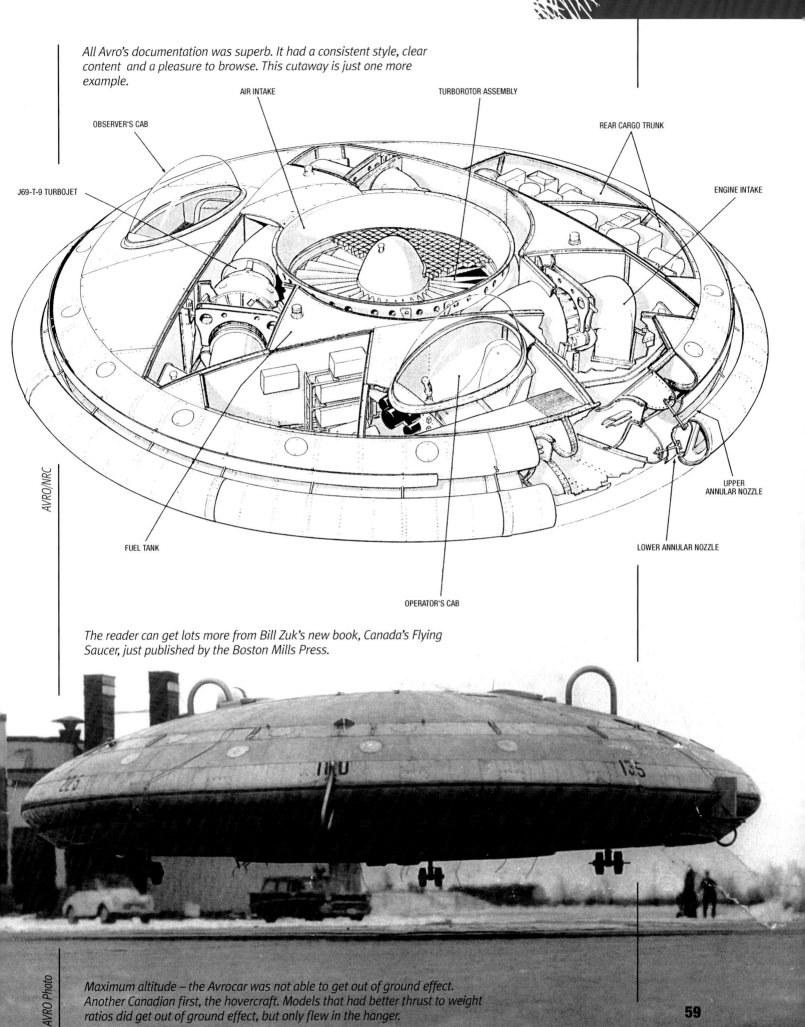

OBSERVER'S CAB

AIR INTAKE

TURBOROTOR ASSEMBLY

REAR CARGO TRUNK

J69-T-9 TURBOJET

ENGINE INTAKE

AVRO/NRC

UPPER
ANNULAR NOZZLE

FUEL TANK

LOWER ANNULAR NOZZLE

OPERATOR'S CAB

The reader can get lots more from Bill Zuk's new book, Canada's Flying Saucer, just published by the Boston Mills Press.

AVRO Photo

Maximum altitude – the Avrocar was not able to get out of ground effect. Another Canadian first, the hovercraft. Models that had better thrust to weight ratios did get out of ground effect, but only flew in the hanger.

59

Avro and Orenda...
after hours

Orenda employees enjoying themselves after work. Earle Brownridge, sixth from the right, was very well respected by all. He started as a time keeper and was clearly one of the everyday workers at the beginning of his career. Rising through the organization to become Vice President and General Manager would be much more difficult today. Have we lost something?

Orenda Photo

The Avro and Orenda recreation clubs were very active. Hockey, golf, and bowling were the top sport interests. The annual picnics and Christmas parties were annual highlights and extremely well attended. Look at the prices!

Avro-Orenda rivalries were settled before Canadair was taken on. Each tournament had a lucky draw for a car. Lorna Dopson poses with a 1957 Meteor.

Orenda/Avro rivalry was matched with the annual A.V. Roe Canada Ltd. vs Canadair hockey tournament. It was a big event. Maple Leaf Gardens was packed with more than 10,000 spectators. The door prizes were generous, with the top one being a new car. On this particular occasion, company executives from Sir Roy Dobson down are present. Crawford Gordon's daughter Cynthia is on hand with a friend. Can you pick out Fred Smye and Earle Brownridge? How about retired Air Marshall Curtis? First lower right, Thor Stephenson, Director Aircraft Division Department of Defence Production. Sitting third from right, J.G. Notman, Canadair President.

A.V. Roe Canada Limited

AVRO Newsmagazine

61

***Arrow** Countdown*

BOMARC and Avro
Was Avro thinking of manufacturing the Bomarc under licence in the mid-fifties?

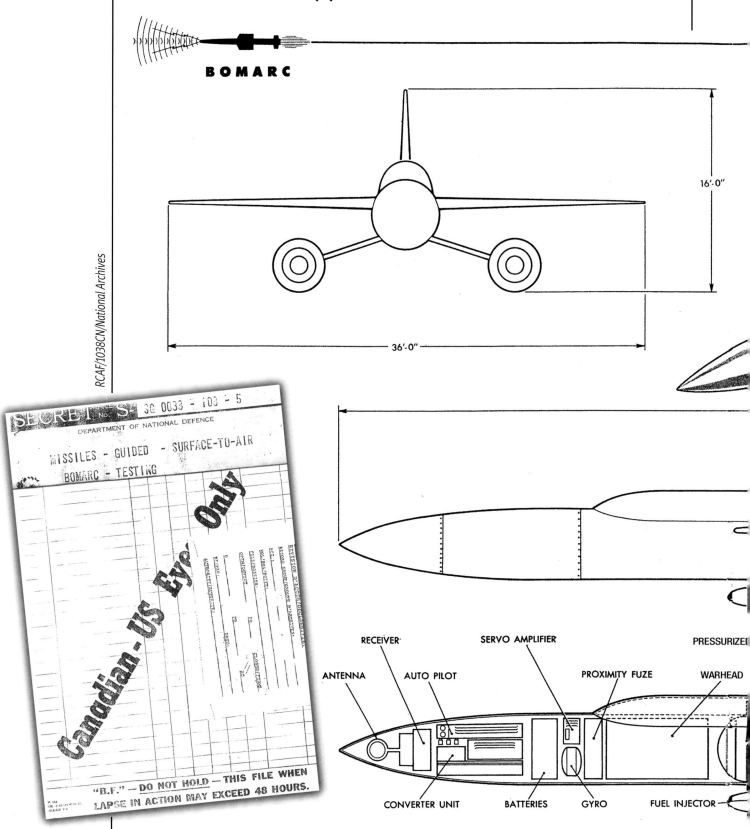

RCAF/1038CN/National Archives

Any serious discussion of the Bomarc is still hidden behind Canadian/US-Eyes-Only classified documentation. Again, one can find the cover but not the content.

"BOMARC" SURFACE TO AIR GUIDED M

AVRO AIRCRAFT LIMITED

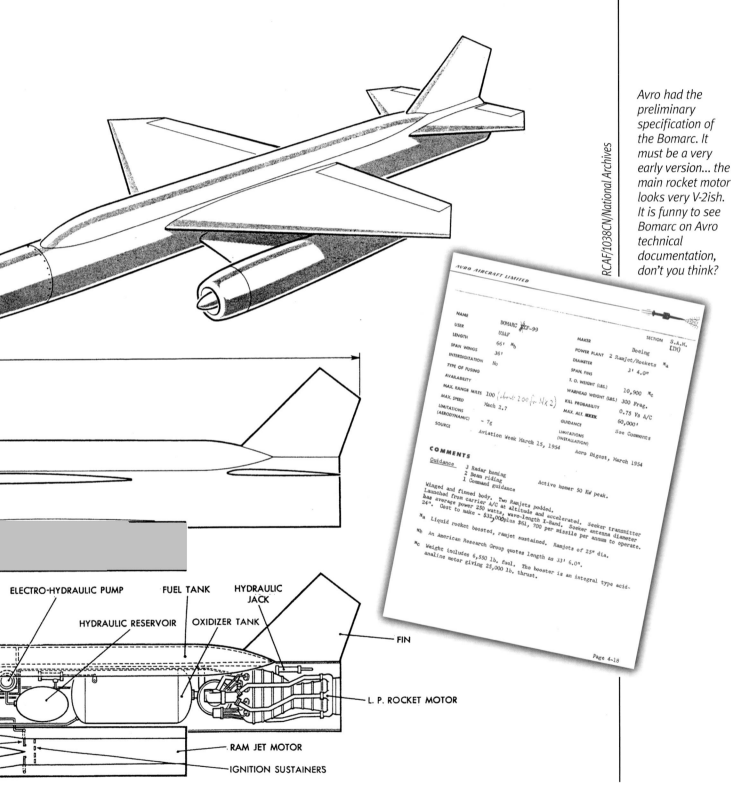

Avro had the preliminary specification of the Bomarc. It must be a very early version... the main rocket motor looks very V-2ish. It is funny to see Bomarc on Avro technical documentation, don't you think?

AVRO AIRCRAFT LIMITED

NAME				
USER	BOMARC XXF-99			SECTION S.A.M. (IM)
LENGTH	USAF	MAKER		
SPAN WINGS	66' Mb	POWER PLANT 2 RamJet/Rockets	Boeing	Ma
INTERDIGITATION	36'	DIAMETER		
TYPE OF FUSING	No	SPAN, FINS	3' 4.0"	
AVAILABILITY		T. O. WEIGHT (LBS.)	10,900	Mc
MAX. RANGE MILES	100 (about 200 for MK 2)	WARHEAD WEIGHT (LBS.)	300 Frag.	
MAX. SPEED	Mach 2.7	KILL PROBABILITY	0.75 Vs A/C	
LIMITATIONS (AERODYNAMIC)	- 7g	MAX. ALT.	60,000'	
SOURCE	Aviation Week March 15, 1954	GUIDANCE	See Comments	
		LIMITATIONS (INSTALLATION)	Aero Digest, March 1954	

COMMENTS

Guidance   3 Radar homing
            2 Beam riding   Active homer 50 KW peak.
            1 Command guidance

Winged and finned body. Two Ramjets podded.
Launched from carrier A/C at altitude and accelerated. Seeker transmitter
has average power 250 watts, wave-length X-Band. Seeker antenna diameter
24". Cost to make - $32,000 plus $61, 700 per missile per annum to operate.

Ma Liquid rocket boosted, ramjet sustained. Ramjets of 25" dia.

Mb An American Research Group quotes length as 33' 6.0".

Mc Weight includes 6,550 lb. fuel. The booster is an integral type acid-
aniline motor giving 25,000 lb. thrust.

Page 4-18

ELECTRO-HYDRAULIC PUMP   FUEL TANK   HYDRAULIC JACK

HYDRAULIC RESERVOIR   OXIDIZER TANK

FIN

L. P. ROCKET MOTOR

RAM JET MOTOR

IGNITION SUSTAINERS

AVRO Canada News

Who was Audrey Underwood?

The CBC mini-series on the Arrow raised Crawford Gorden's alleged affair with his long time private secretary Audrey Underwood. In the January 1952 issue of 'Avro Canada News,' Audrey was featured in the Personality on Parade section authored by Fred Lawrence. He reports that she was with Gordon while he worked for C.D. Howe , with him at the John Inglis Company, with him at the English Electric Company and still with him at A.V. Roe Canada Ltd. The article told of her dynamic personality and match-up with Crawford Gordon. In Creig Stewart's Arrow Through the Heart, Audrey is pegged as wanting to move on in 1952. Her going-away party at Avro attests to her popularity and power. She obviously had a strong connection to Gordon, to have stayed with him for many years and to not marry until after his death in the sixties. She died within a few years, in the US, of a stray bullet wound to the head as a result of a bizarre neighbourhood shooting.

AVRO Newsmagazine

Avro Canada executive secretaries getting together at the King Edward Hotel, 1951. These gals kept the place humming.

1. Joyce Williams
2. Jean Williams
3. June Armstrong
4. Kay Rumble
5. Marilyn Watkins
6. Dorothy Riley
7. Mary Kelly
8. Jolaine McKee
9. Bep Pott
10. June Daliner
11. Mima Kirk
12. Hazel Canning
13. Shirley Stolberg

14. Myrtle Carruthers
15. Edith MacDonald
16. Lucy Hacking
17. Jordy Campbell
18. Margaret Madison
19. Lila Forest
20. Anne Coates
21. Shirley Munshaw
22. Betty Moore
23. Helen Hicks
24. Jo-Anne Jackson
25. Dora Dainton
26. Jean Janes

27. Lyn Jewett
28. Isabel Batcheller
29. Helen Polyak
30. Norma McGregor
31. Dolores Cunningham
32. Eileen O'Donnell
33. Vera Meade
34. Lucille McGuire
35. Jean Morley
36. Audrey Underwood
37. Helen Bennett
38. Jackie Lascelles

AVRO Newsmagazine

Front Row	Centre Row	Back Row
Jo-Anne Jackson	Doris Bridge	Jo Lindow
Helen grand	Kay Terry	Mary Kelly
Jean Morley	Isabel Batcheller	Dorothy Riley
Audrey Underwood	Jordy Campbell	Dora Dointon
Edith MacDonald	Helen Polyak	Helen Ronald
Clair Bain	Betty Moore	Maureen Mckay
Greta Hoar	Myrtle Haughlon	Bep Pott
Norma McGregor	Lucille Patterson	Lena Benbow
	Elizabeth McGrath	Lois MacMillan
	Helen Bennett	
	Jean Cronie	

When Audrey Underwood left Avro in early 1952, she was celebrated by her peers. With their front row legs showing, at a time when long dresses were in fashion, attractive Avro secretaries pose for her farewell. These are the ladies that made things happen... the power behind the thrones.

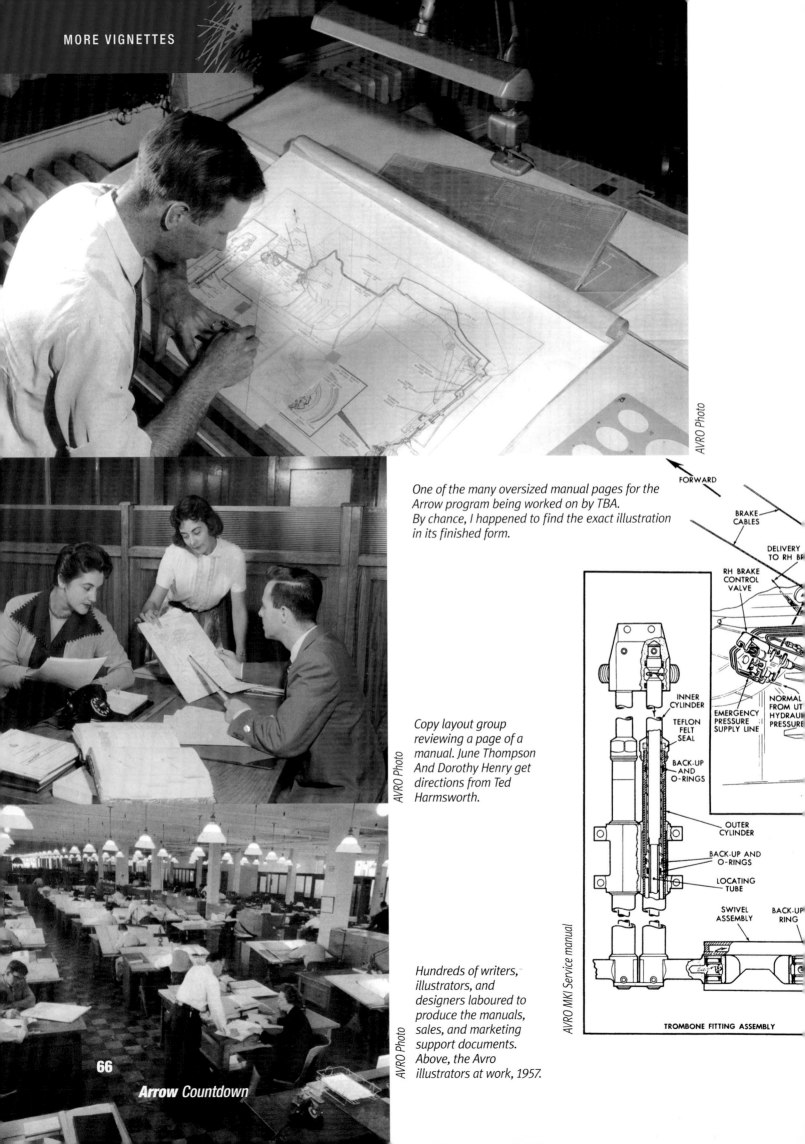

AVRO Photo

One of the many oversized manual pages for the Arrow program being worked on by TBA.
By chance, I happened to find the exact illustration in its finished form.

Copy layout group reviewing a page of a manual. June Thompson And Dorothy Henry get directions from Ted Harmsworth.

AVRO Photo

AVRO Photo

Hundreds of writers, illustrators, and designers laboured to produce the manuals, sales, and marketing support documents. Above, the Avro illustrators at work, 1957.

AVRO MKI Service manual

FORWARD

BRAKE CABLES

DELIVERY TO RH BR

RH BRAKE CONTROL VALVE

INNER CYLINDER

TEFLON FELT SEAL

BACK-UP AND O-RINGS

EMERGENCY PRESSURE SUPPLY LINE

NORMAL FROM UT HYDRAU PRESSURE

OUTER CYLINDER

BACK-UP AND O-RINGS

LOCATING TUBE

SWIVEL ASSEMBLY

BACK-UP RING

TROMBONE FITTING ASSEMBLY

Technical Publications

A tribute to some of the many who contributed to the excellent quality and scope of the Avro/Orenda Publications Department.

In 1955, Avro alone produced more than 5,000 pages of illustrated manuals, supporting its products through the Sales and Service Division headed by Joe Morley.

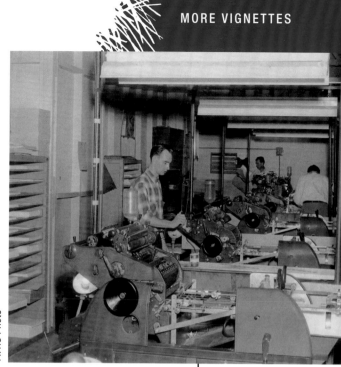

AVRO Photo

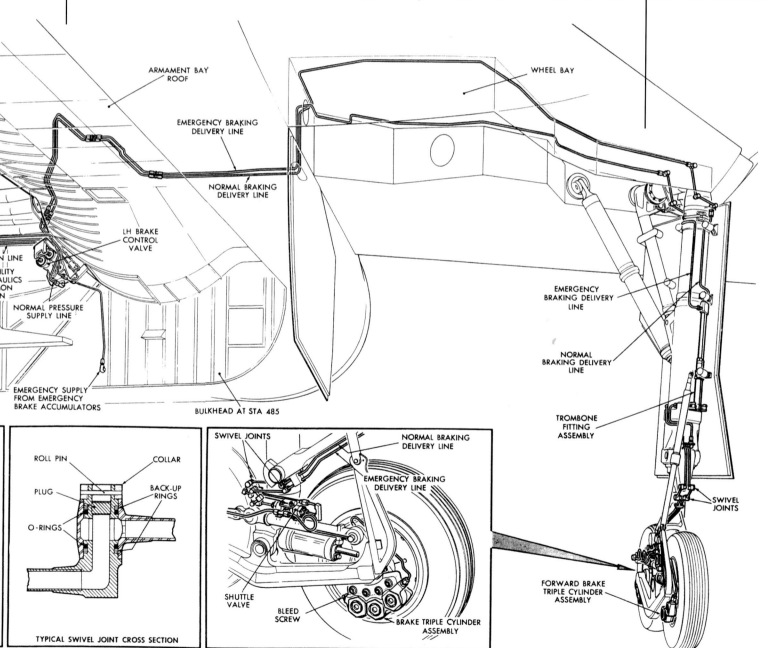

ARMAMENT BAY ROOF

WHEEL BAY

EMERGENCY BRAKING DELIVERY LINE

NORMAL BRAKING DELIVERY LINE

LH BRAKE CONTROL VALVE

N LINE
TILITY
AULICS
MON
N

NORMAL PRESSURE SUPPLY LINE

EMERGENCY SUPPLY FROM EMERGENCY BRAKE ACCUMULATORS

BULKHEAD AT STA 485

EMERGENCY BRAKING DELIVERY LINE

NORMAL BRAKING DELIVERY LINE

TROMBONE FITTING ASSEMBLY

SWIVEL JOINTS

FORWARD BRAKE TRIPLE CYLINDER ASSEMBLY

ROLL PIN

COLLAR

PLUG

BACK-UP RINGS

O-RINGS

TYPICAL SWIVEL JOINT CROSS SECTION

SWIVEL JOINTS

NORMAL BRAKING DELIVERY LINE

EMERGENCY BRAKING DELIVERY LINE

SHUTTLE VALVE

BLEED SCREW

BRAKE TRIPLE CYLINDER ASSEMBLY

Arrow MK II brake hydraulic system illustration. Today, a lot of this work is handled with the help of computers. Then, it was all done by hand... what a tremendous effort!

Arrow Pilots
get USA Delta flight experience albeit with some difficulty!

Jan Zurakowski at the controls of an F102, Delta Dagger. No direct flying at a USAF base was approved in the time frame requested. However, Convair supplied the necessary hardware at their Palmdale facility.

Jan Zurakowski Photo

Group Captain Ray Foottit builds the case for supersonic delta flying experience as being essential for the Arrow programme. Timing is of the essence.

RCAF 1038CN/National Archives

RESTRICTED
1038CN-80(AMTS/DAEng)

MEMORANDUM

DGT

CF105 Aircraft
Supersonic Flying Training for AVRO Test Pilots   18 Jul 56

1   Reference is made to telecon G/C Carling Kelly - G/C Foottit regarding the cancellation by DGT of our request to CJS (Wash) ref S1038CN-180(CAE) dated 20 Jun 56, that an indoctrination course in flying supersonic aircraft be obtained for three Avro Aircraft Ltd. test pilots.

2   During discussion between A/V/M Hendrick, A/C Truscott and Mr. Syme, General Manager of Avro Aircraft Limited on 12 Jun 56 it was requested by Mr. Syme and agreed that the RCAF would facilitate the arrangements of such a course with the USAF. Mr. Syme confirmed his request by letter to CAE on 13 Jun 56 and has reconfirmed the request by telecon on 17 Jul 56.

3   Such a course for the Avro test pilots is vital to the CF105 development program. By giving the test pilots experience in flying supersonic aircraft the risk involved in the initial development flying of the CF105 will be reduced and therefore the heavy investment that the RCAF has in the aircraft will be protected. In addition, experience in flying supersonic aircraft other than the CF105 will give the Avro test pilots a broader background against which they will be able to assess and criticize the characteristic of the CF105. This will help insure that the RCAF gets a better product.

4   The pilots are Messrs. J. Zurakowski, P.R. Cope and W.J. Potocki. The first two have been cleared to "SECRET" and clearances are being processed at the present time for Mr. Potocki.

5   The basic aim of the requested course is to give the pilots a thorough grounding in flying supersonic aircraft with as diversified experience as possible. In particular, experience in flying the F102 would be most applicable because of its similar configuration to the CF105. It would be preferable to train the pilots in sequence starting with Mr. Zurakowski, during the period from 1 Sept 56 to 1 Apr 57.

6   In view of your statement that sponsorship of such a USAF course will cost the RCAF a large amount of money, may a costing of the desired course be made and the information forwarded to DAEng as soon as possible.

(H.R. Foottit) G/C
DAEng
(2-5485)

61027

61014

FC

U.S

CANOPY LATCH MECHANISM &
& BRAKE CONTROL CYL.

SECRET
S1038CN-180 (DGT)

PA - SCR.

MEMORANDUM

23 Oct 56

CAE

CF105 Aircraft
Supersonic Flying Experience for AVRO Test Pilots

1   Reference your S1038CN-180 (AMTS/CAE) dated 11 Oct 56, the following action has been taken in an attempt to obtain supersonic flying experience for AVRO test pilots:

(a)   On 23 Jul CJS Washington was requested to provide this Headquarters with cost of giving three civilian test pilots ten hours flying experience each on a USAF Supersonic aircraft, preferably the F 102.

(b)   On 28 Aug CJS Washington advised that the USAF would be unable to provide F 102 flying until 1958. They suggested that such flying might be obtained from the factory if Supersonic Delta Wing experience was a prime requirement.

DA Eng.
Toronto.

(c)   On 29 Aug telecom from this Headquarters instructed CJS Washington to open immediate negotiations with the factory.

(d)   On 17 Oct CJS Washington advised that a formal approach has now been made through Headquarters USAF requesting:

(i)   Two to five hour flight experience on production F 102A at Convair Facility Palmdale, California.

(ii)   Permission to discuss characteristics of Supersonic Delta Wing aircraft with Convair Chief Experimental Test Pilot and an appropriate USAF officer at USAF Flight Center and at Air Proving Ground Command.

(iii)   A 60 day period commencing 1 Feb 57 was requested.

2   It is agreed that Supersonic Delta Wing test flying is of prime importance to the AVRO test pilot. However, because of the present state of Delta Wing flying in the US this is very difficult to obtain. Because of previous informal negotiations CJS Washington anticipate a favourable reply to the formal request made to the USAF on 30 Aug 56.

(V H Patriarche) A/C
CTrain

SECRET
S1038CN-180(AMTS/CAE)

MEMORANDUM

C/Train

11 Oct 56

CF105 Aircraft
Supersonic Flying Experience for AVRO Test Pilots

1   On the 12 June 56, AMTS, Mr. Smye President of AVRO Aircraft and myself agreed that supersonic flying experience for the AVRO test pilots was of prime importance to the development of the aircraft and that the RCAF would facilitate arrangements with the USAF for this flying. In accordance with this agreement CJS (Wash) were instructed to take this matter up with the USAF.

2   On the 16 Jul 56 it was discovered that DGT had instructed CJS (Wash) to cancel my request regarding supersonic flying experience for the AVRO pilots. Subsequent conversation between DAEng and DGT revealed that DGT was concerned about the high cost to the RCAF for flying USAF aircraft. DAEng memorandum to DGT ref. S1038CN-180 dated 16 Jul 56 requested that an immediate costing of the required flying time be obtained. While DAEng's memorandum has not been answered, verbal information from DGT indicates that negotiations with the USAF have been unsuccessful in that supersonic flying time on the F102 will not be available until 1958, long past the scheduled first flight of the CF105 in May 57.

3   Four months have elapsed since the agreement was reached to facilitate supersonic flying experience for AVRO test pilots. The results to date are unsatisfactory. Only 6½ months remain before the CF105 is scheduled to fly. During this time negotiations with the USAF must be brought to a successful conclusion, visit clearances for the AVRO pilots must be arranged, and the actual flying must take place. It is therefore requested that priority be placed on the negotiations to obtain supersonic flying experience for the AVRO test pilots.

(G.G. Truscott) A/C
CAE

DEPARTMENT OF NATIONAL DEFENCE
MESSAGE FORM
FOR CLASSIFIED MESSAGES ONLY

INDICATE DEGREE OF PRECEDENCE	FOR MESSAGE CENTRE USE ONLY	MARK X TO INDICATE SECURITY CLASSIFICATION	
	SCR	TOPSEC	
OPERATIONAL IMMEDIATE		SECRET	X
PRIORITY	X	CONFD	
ROUTINE	X		RESTD	
IF NOT MARKED WILL BE TRANSMITTED DEFERRED	FROM CANAIRHED	GR	
	TO CANAIRDEF		

INFO

ORIGINATOR'S NO.
OR 347

ATTENTION S&SO. THE USAF HAVE TENTATIVELY APPROVED TWO RCAF PILOTS PARTICIPATING IN THE OPERATIONAL SUITABILITY TESTS OF THE CONVAIR 102A. THESE TESTS WILL TAKE PLACE AT EGLIN AIR FORCE BASE COMMENCING APPROXIMATELY JANUARY 56 AND LASTING ABOUT SIX MONTHS. THIS AIRCRAFT CARRIES EQUIPMENT SIMILAR TO THAT WHICH IS TO BE FITTED TO THE CF 105 AND CONSEQUENTLY THIS OFFER WOULD GIVE US AN EXCELLENT OPPORTUNITY TO MAKE AN EARLY ASSESSMENT OF SUCH EQUIPMENT. IT HAS BEEN DECIDED THEREFORE THAT ONE PILOT OF S/L OR SENIOR F/L RANK SHOULD PARTICIPATE FROM ADC THE OTHER PILOT WILL BE SELECTED FROM CEPE. IN VIEW OF IMPORTANCE OF THESE TESTS TO THE RCAF IT IS NECESSARY THAT THE PILOT SELECTED BY ADC BE HIGHLY QUALIFIED IN ALL WEATHER OPERATIONS AND CURRENT AS REGARD JET FLYING. ADVISE THIS HEADQUARTERS AS SOON AS POSSIBLE OF NAME OF SELECTED OFFICER.

ORIGINATOR		TELEPHONE	DATE - TIME GROUP		FILE NO.
(JRD BRAHAM) W/C	OR 3	7104	26 SEP 55	Z	S1038CF105-180

MESSAGE CENTRE COPY

RCAF 1038CN/National Archives

Frustration with approval delays and internal communication difficulties give rise to this internal DND memorandum. Note that the Arrow's first flight was envisioned for spring 1957... it didn't happen until a year later, March 25, 1958.

The RCAF is also getting delta flying experience... but seems to have less trouble!

Final approval was received in the fall of 1956, a full year after the first negotiations started.

Avro Vulcans visit
Malton for 1958 CNE Airshow fly-by

RCAF Photo

RCAF Photo

The Avro Group look is reflected in the livery of the parked Vulcans and RL202 on Avro's Malton taxi-way. Clear differences between subsonic and supersonic wings are in evidence. Look at the thickness of the the Vulcan wings!

Visiting RAF Vulcan pilots chat at the foot of RL202. "Spud" Potocki, now Avro's Chief Test Pilot explains the cockpit layout to one of the RAF officers. Unfortunately, the Arrow didn't fly at the airshow due to bad weather. We all missed out on this one. I do remember the Vulcans. The ground shuddered with the roar of their accelerated fly-by. Very impressive.

Thousands of people packed the Canadian National Exhibition waterfront during the 1958 Labour Day weekend. They saw aviation history when the giant Vulcan bombers came over the Toronto skyscape from lake Ontario. I remember being there, and in awe of the thunder and might of these beauties. Little did I realize that I would be involved 40 years later with bringing back some thunder of our own. The bombers had been seen at different airshows on either side of the Atlantic,

on one flight, on the very same day. Taking off from the 1958 SBAC Air Show at Farnborough UK, at 2:50 British time, they flew over the air show in Toronto 61/2 hours later at about 4:30 local time. What a thrill. The crowd was disappointed however, because the Arrow which had ben scheduled to fly never made it... something about weather... I don't remember it being bad, do you?

Avro flight test hosted the RAF Vulcan crews. In front of RL202, from left to right, F/O John Ward, Don Rogers (Avro), S/L Donald Skeen, "Spud" Potocki (Avro), F/L Alex Bowie, F/O Ben Harris, and F/L Henry Swan. The 1958 Canadian National Exhibition air display and air exhibits were a prelude celebration to the 100th anniversary of Canadian powered flight, the following year.

RCAF Photo

AVRO
AIRCRAFT

Avro

MARCH, 1959
VOL. 5, NO. 4

Special
Supplement

NEWSMAGAZINE

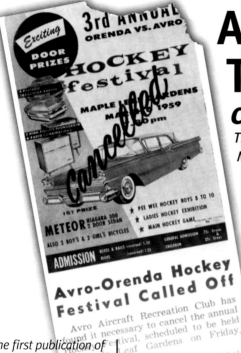

The first publication of Avro Newsmagazine after the Arrow programme cancellation is revealing in that it puts a brave face on what was, in reality, an unmitigated disaster. In speaking to John Plant about a year ago, he told me that Avro management had an idea of the government's intentions and warned them that massive layoffs would result if the programme was going to be cancelled. This was not vindictive but rather practical because of seniority complications with the unions involved. There were no surprises in reality. Cancelling the hockey tournament was understandable.

Arrow Program Terminated

Company To Carry On, President Reports

The following message is directed by Mr. J. L. Plant, President and General Manager, to Avro personnel:

At this writing, a total of some 1600 personnel are back at work at Avro on contracts remaining after the Government's cancellation of the Arrow program.

Weekly and hourly paid personnel who have returned to work were recalled on the basis of their seniority in occupational groups and in accordance with the terms of the Collective Agreements with the Company's Unions.

They form the nucleus of the company we are endeavouring to reorganize on the foundation of the Avro we have known over the past years.

It is gratifying to note the dispatch with which the re-hiring of personnel was made possible by the dedicated Avroites, who virtually worked the clock around in order to give every possible attention to their task. It is also encouraging to note the complete co-operation in this matter from the National Employment Service. Without this concentration of effort by all concerned we would still be engaged in the great mass of detail that is obviously associated with the termination of employment of some 9,000 people, and an effort to re-employ as many as possible in the shortest possible time.

The government order to terminate all work on the Arrow program came to us suddenly. A rumor started around the factory that the Arrow program had been terminated. Later, we learned that this rumor emanated from radio bulletins.

On confirming the truth and fact of these radio reports from the representative at Avro of the Department of Defence Production, Mr. C. A. Hore, it became imperative that I advise the company's personnel of this development.

When I sat down in front of the company's Public Address system microphone in the little brick building opposite Gate 9 to announce the Arrow cancellation, it was one of the toughest jobs I've ever undertaken. How do you tell some 9,000 people that the job they have been dedicated to, for years, has been cancelled? How do you tell them that the product of their minds and hands has been eliminated?

These were my remarks:

"The radio has recently announced the Prime Minister has stated in the House of Commons this morning that the Avro Arrow and Iroquois programs have been terminated.

We, the management of the company had no official information prior to this announcement being made. The cancellation of the Arrow and the Iroquois has, however, been confirmed as a fact by Mr. C. A. Hore, the representative here of the Department of Defence Production.

It is impossible at this stage to give you any further details until such time as I receive the official telegram from Ottawa. In the meantime I would ask that you continue with your work. Later on in the day you will be informed as to our future. Thank you."

As the morning of the contract termination progressed into early afternoon, it became apparent that the first step to be taken was to give notice of termination to all workers, and then recall those who would be required on remaining contracts after the cancellation of the Arrow, in accordance with our Collective Agreements with the Unions.

72

With regard to engineers and other administrative personnel not subject to Union Agreements, every effort is being made by the company to utilize their services wherever possible.

A large portion of the engineering team is no longer required for work on existing programs and, despite efforts to maintain a nucleus of this team, a very large number cannot be re-employed at this time. The Company is endeavoring to obtain employment for them in other Canadian industries, with the hope that many of them may be recalled by Avro if suitable projects can be built up in the future.

In addition, the company is negotiating with American companies in an endeavor to place out groups of our staff on a subcontract basis for short periods of time, in the hope that many of them can also be recalled in the future.

It is hoped, in this way, to provide re-employment for as many Canadian engineers as possible to companies who are in need of their particular skills, and the scheme should also provide opportunity for Canadian engineers to obtain additional experience on advanced aeronautical-space projects.

The ability of the Avro engineering team has been universally recognized, and the future success of Avro's technical accomplishments will depend on its ability to retain as much of the main structure of this team as possible. This is what the Company is endeavoring to do.

The telegram received from the government that officially terminated the Arrow contracts included these instructions:

"Take notice that your contracts bearing the reference numbers set out below including all amendments hereto are terminated as regards all supplies and services which have not been completed and shipped or performed thereunder prior to the receipt by you of this notice. You shall cease all work immediately, terminate subcontracts and orders, place no further subcontracts or orders and instruct all your subcontractors and suppliers to take similar action.

With this firm instruction to immediately cancel all work on the Arrow, there was no more work for those personnel engaged on that project. They could not and would not want to just stand around. And how was a snap judgment to be made as to who worked on Arrow and who did not – and who had necessary seniority – and so on? Thus came about the decision for the abrupt notice of termination for all personnel.

National Archives

In a statement to the House of Commons exactly one week later, on February 27, with regard to discussions between the Government and senior officials of A. V. Roe Canada Limited, the Hon. Donald Fleming, Minister of Finance, stated in part: 'It is the hope of the Government and the companies that (these) combined efforts will result in a steady increase in employment."

This is indeed the hope and, in fact, the determination of Avro and I am very sure, of Orenda as well. Because Avro and Orenda have proven their capabilities on an international scale and have no intention of permitting this capability to wither and die.

At the moment the main projects that remain for Avro are:

1. Repair and overhaul of CF-100s in NATO service in Canada and Europe.
2. Development of Avro's vertical take off vehicles' family in conjunction with the United States government.

It could be said that the "new Avro" is being reorganized around these two projects and that the future will indicate the extent of the company's possible expansion of work and employment.

Sincerely,
J. L. Plant.

Boat hulls made by Avro Aircraft? You bet... just one of the attempts to find work for the much diminished capacity of the Malton plant. The design department explored many options. By 1962 Avro Aircraft would find no support for their ideas. The company effectively ceased to exist and was wound up. Even A.V. Roe Canada Ltd. became Hawker Siddeley Canada.

ANON

ANON

Arrows Waiting For Cutup

Right after cancellation, the first five MKI Arrows were pulled into the Experimental Hanger. RL201 is being stripped. Ground handling equipment and fixtures are stacked along the north wall... no one has yet decided what is to become of these beauties. All five are definetly accounted for at this time. Nothing got away as was rumored the day after "black" Friday. In fact, the wooden mock-up is even present at the west end of the building.

RL 201

From the underside of RL205, it is clear that RL201 is already being stripped. The Pratt & Whitney J75 engine has been pulled out. You can see it near the north wall of the hangar. RL204 sits majestically awaiting its fate. RL203 and 204 are being kept at the ready in case the talked about transfer to the UK's Royal Aeronautical Establishment are finalized.

EMERGENCY CANOPY OPENING OTHER SIDE

ANON

RL 204

Arrow Countdown

ANON

Death Row Walk About...

The Place, the west side of the Avro experimental building. At the end of May 1959, inquiries for use of the Arrow by the RAE, UK, appeared to have been terminated. It's time to start dismantling. You are there! Interestingly, no paper trail of the negotiations has ever surfaced. The pictures speak for themselves.

RL201 is dismantled with the left elevator removed. Air conditioning equipment is being accessed and removed. Before cut-up, it appears that all the planes were stripped of useful items as per the RCAF's instructions to the Department of Defence Production. The CF-100 in the background survived. Another J75 from RL204 is just visible by the RL201's fin.

ANON

25201

ANON

Arrow *Countdown*

What a view of RL205. It really does look like a production item, brand new with only 40 minutes on the air frame. Some dismantling is taking place... the weapons pack and the Martin-Baker ejection seats. Clam shell doors and associated mechanism are clearly visible.

Herb Nott, June 24, 1959

One of the first shots of Herb Nott's famous footage on June 24, 1959 as he flies over the Avro plant in an unauthorized flight. You are looking east. We can see the four remaining Arrows on death row just in front of the Experimental building. To the north is the Fuel System Rig building. It appears to be used for the scrappers. In the background is the #1 Orenda Engines plant, where the Iroquois was being built. Just to the right is the new High Altitude Test Facility, now a Bingo Hall, and above that the newly built engine test cells. The rest of Orenda Engines is seen at the top of the picture. J75 engine cans can be seen on the extreme left. I have pored over this photo to look for traces of RL202... none found!

Arrow Files to the NRC
More background on how the National Research Council, NAE library, acquired the largest single find of Arrow/Iroquois files

CABLE ADDRESS "RESEARCH"

IN YOUR REPLY PLEASE QUOTE

FILE No.....................................

NATIONAL RESEARCH COUNCIL
CANADA

DIVISION OF MECHANICAL ENGINEERING
OFFICE OF THE DIRECTOR

OTTAWA 2, 8 June 1961

Air Vice Marshal J. A. Easton,
Air Member for Technical Services,
Royal Canadian Air Force,
Department of National Defence,
125 Elgin Street,
Ottawa, Ontario.

Dear Air Vice Marshal Easton:

Avro Arrow Reports

As you are perhaps aware, we have had some discussions with your people (in particular with Flight Lieutenant R. P. Williams) concerning the possibility of our looking after the various reports on the Avro Arrow aircraft. Although we should be glad to do this if you wish us to, there are two or three problems on which we should need some assistance, namely:-

a) Since I understand that many of the reports are progress reports leading to final reports, we should like the assistance of someone with the discretion and the authority to weed out the progress reports whose substance is covered later. We believe that this procedure would in any case greatly enhance the value of the collection.

b) It would be advantageous to downgrade the security classification of the reports as far as possible, so that they need not all be housed in a security storage.

c) Since we are ourselves in a somewhat tight position in the Library concerning cataloguing, etc., some assistance in the recording and cataloguing would be appreciated. Otherwise there may be a considerable delay before records are available.

With the above kinds of problems in mind we should nevertheless be very pleased to see to the preservation of these important documents if you want us to.

Yours very truly,

D. C. MacPhail,
Director.

DCM/JVT

Right after cancellation, RCAF personnel started wondering what would become of the large volume of data accumulated over many years. Natural gathering points were the libraries within specific units such as AMTS and the RCAF headquarters Technical Library. Within a few months, it became apparent that they were in fact dead files and took up major footage of shelf space. Their natural resting place was either the incinerator or an institution, suitably classified, of a national character, and related to aviation. The National Aeronautical Establishment, part of the the NRC filled the bill as their director indicates.

MINUTE SHEET

Min (1)

AMTS

1   Elimination of all Arrow reports is part of a broad
programme to weed out obsolete and/or little used material and bring
some order to the present chaotic state of the AFHQ Technical
Library. This covers some 1500 documents held in the library, CEPE
and 1102. TSD.

2   Our discussion with the NAE library staff was based on
the following points:

    (a)   The present library space will not permit the
        luxury of holding publications of doubtful value
        to our present work and as such would have to
        be destroyed or placed in dead storage.

    (b)   Certain Arrow documents may have basic research
        value and if possible should be made available
        to Canadian industry generally. The NAE
        library because of its national position would
        appear to be the logical home for these documents
        provided of course their facilities would permit
        this fairly substantial listing.

3   Their staff fully supported this proposal and in fact
felt it was an excellent opportunity to supplement their present
meagre holdings of this weapon system.

4   With specific reference to Dr. McPhail's letter it is
pointed out that:

    (a)   the board of officers presently established to
        screen the AFHQ Library holdings could carry out
        this function.

    (b)   It is doubtful if many reports would still require
        a security classification. This should not present
        any problem.

    (c)   Our present library staff is under-established and
        have a considerable backlog of work. Assistance
        to the NAE Library could be provided but would
        add to our present difficulties.

                                  (GM Sutherland) S/L
                                  AEM 2
                                (2-0685)

14 Jun 61

*This document was meant to inform AMTS, Air Member for Technical Services, namely AVM Easton, of the
Arrow files dilemma. Yes, this is the same Easton missile man, who was alleged to have been the prime
mover in stopping the Arrow program and having had some hand in its infamous disposal. His feelings
certainly appear different with respect to Arrow files disposal. I received a note from Easton's grandson who
was perplexed with the Arrow Scrapbook's indication that his grandfather had something to do with the
Arrow's demise. He said that the cancellation of the Arrow was the reason for AVM Easton's unhappy early
retirement from the RCAF only a couple of years after the Arrow's fall. There is more to uncover... for sure!*

It is quite clear that AVM Easton is very supportive of ensuring some continuity of information. Although the general principle was established that RCAF, Arrow files would be consolidated and transferred to the NRC Aeronautical library many locations were not included or consulted. For example, all files relating to the Arrow electronic systems were consolidated and transferred to Rockcliffe dead storage in the Directorate of Engineering. They have never been found and with the recent closure of CFB Rockcliff all files have been moved, no one seems to know where, possibly to the National Archives or to DHIST&HER, DND's Directorate of History and Heritage or for disposal, Heaven forbid.

RCAF 1038CN/National Archives

10380N-60(AAEM)

Ottawa, Ontario.

JUN 16 1961

Office of the Director,
National Aeronautical Establishment,
National Research Council,
Montreal Road, Ottawa,
Ontario.

Dear Dr. MacPhail:

Re: AVRO Arrow Reports

I thank you for your letter of the 15th June covering the above noted subject. We would be most pleased if you would accept receipt of these reports into your library.

As you know our library space problems have been very acute for some time. The holding of documents such as Arrow reports, which now have only an historical or research value, tend to compound our problems. Owing to the national position of the NAE library however, these documents would be available to a wider group in the aeronautical field hence their value would be enhanced.

The points covered in para (a) and (b) of your letter, namely the telescoping of files and security downgrading, will be carried out. Para (c) presents a problem to us since our library is already under-established. However, consideration can be given to loaning a civilian clerk-typist who has had some experience with the Arrow files. The exact timing of her move and the extent of her duties would have to be known in advance since her absence from the AMTS/CAE Typing Pool during the critical summer holiday season could present further difficulties.

The administration of our library is handled by the Assistant for Aeronautical Engineering Management (AEM2), S/L G.M. Sutherland (Local 2-0685), and detailed arrangements required to complete the transfer of these documents will be co-ordinated by this office.

Once again, thank you for your kind assistance on this problem.

Yours very truly,

(SGD) J. A. EASTON A/V/M

(J.A. Easton)
Air Vice Marshal
for Chief of the Air Staff

F/L DC Williams/MVB
2-0548
AMTS
CAE
Orig
Circ
Loc
File

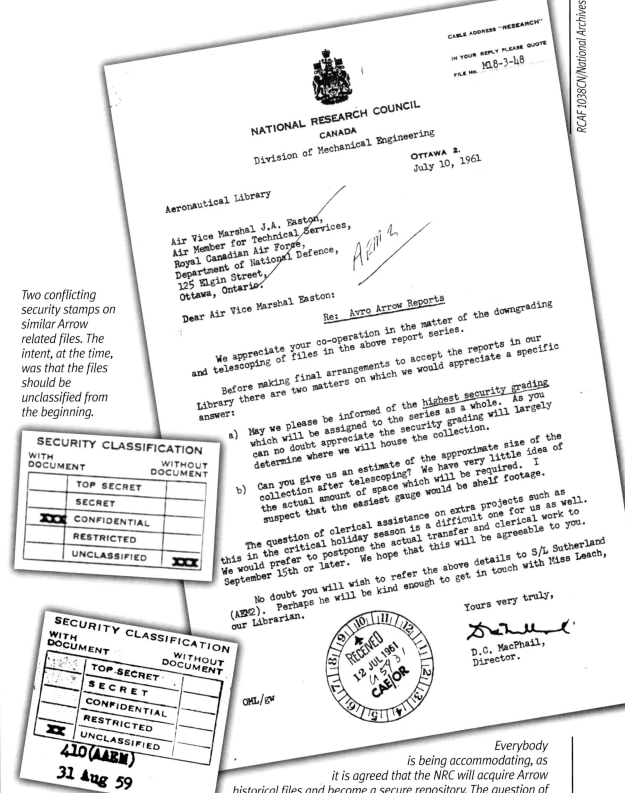

CABLE ADDRESS "RESEARCH"

IN YOUR REPLY PLEASE QUOTE

FILE No. M18-3-48

NATIONAL RESEARCH COUNCIL

CANADA

Division of Mechanical Engineering

OTTAWA 2.
July 10, 1961

Aeronautical Library

Air Vice Marshal J.A. Easton,
Air Member for Technical Services,
Royal Canadian Air Force,
Department of National Defence,
125 Elgin Street,
Ottawa, Ontario.

Dear Air Vice Marshal Easton:

Re: Avro Arrow Reports

We appreciate your co-operation in the matter of the downgrading
and telescoping of files in the above report series.

Before making final arrangements to accept the reports in our
Library there are two matters on which we would appreciate a specific
answer:

a) May we please be informed of the highest security grading
which will be assigned to the series as a whole. As you
can no doubt appreciate the security grading will largely
determine where we will house the collection.

b) Can you give us an estimate of the approximate size of the
collection after telescoping? We have very little idea of
the actual amount of space which will be required. I
suspect that the easiest gauge would be shelf footage.

The question of clerical assistance on extra projects such as
this in the critical holiday season is a difficult one for us as well.
We would prefer to postpone the actual transfer and clerical work to
September 15th or later. We hope that this will be agreeable to you.

No doubt you will wish to refer the above details to S/L Sutherland
(AEM2). Perhaps he will be kind enough to get in touch with Miss Leach,
our Librarian.

Yours very truly,

D.C. MacPhail,
Director.

OML/gw

RECEIVED
12 JUL 1961
CAE/OR

Two conflicting
security stamps on
similar Arrow
related files. The
intent, at the time,
was that the files
should be
unclassified from
the beginning.

SECURITY CLASSIFICATION

	WITH DOCUMENT	WITHOUT DOCUMENT
TOP SECRET		
SECRET		
CONFIDENTIAL	XXX	
RESTRICTED		
UNCLASSIFIED		XXX

SECURITY CLASSIFICATION

	WITH DOCUMENT	WITHOUT DOCUMENT
TOP SECRET		
SECRET		
CONFIDENTIAL		
RESTRICTED		
UNCLASSIFIED	XX	

410 (AAEM)

31 Aug 59

*Everybody
is being accommodating, as
it is agreed that the NRC will acquire Arrow
historical files and become a secure repository. The question of
security classification is an interesting one, and, as shown by
the two classification stamps, both from similar Arrow related
files, one is marked 'confidential' while the other is marked 'unclassified.' When Arrow interest was
resurrected in the early eighties and because the files were stored in a secure vault they somehow
were not unclassified. Considerable work is required to get files declassified. A freedom of information
application is made. Report titles are not classified but contents are! A subject matter expert is needed
to determine the contents sensitivity. If a foreign power is involved, such as the USA in the case of the
Arrow, they must be consulted and sign off for information release. Time consuming and difficult. It
was done for most of the NRC files through the DND Directorate of Scientific Information Systems, by
Barb Aubrey. Many files remain... there is no global exemption granted ... as yet!*

J-75 Slush Fund

At the end of the Arrow programme, 19 J-75 engines had been bought from Pratt & Whitney US via the USAF to be used in the MKI Arrows. There were four P-3 prototypes and 15 P-5 production models. After protracted negotiations lasting nearly 2 years, a deal was struck.

With less than 70 hours of flight operations on all these engines they were sold back to the USAF for about $2 million dollars, about 25% of the original price. The money did not go back to the Department of Defence Production but rather directly to the RCAF, to be used at their discretion in a year that saw a number of cutbacks.

Pratt & Whitney

A view of the J-75, with the afterburner attached, as it was fitted into the MKI Arrow. It arrived in two Rheems containers one for the engine, the other for the afterburner. It was longer, 1500 lbs. heavier, and produced 40% less thrust than the Iroquois, the Arrow MK II engine, under development at Orenda Engines Ltd.

This telex removed the 19 J-75 engines from the RCAF roll and paved the way for their eventual sale.

RCAF 1038CN/National Archives

1038CN-80

MEMORANDUM

AUG 10 1960

9 August 1960

THE MINISTER

Disposal of J75 Engines

1.   At the termination of the Arrow programme the RCAF
had for disposal 4 J75P3 prototype and 15 J75P5 production
engines which had been bought for installation in pre-production
Arrow aircraft.

2.   USAF has now agreed to buy back these engines plus
related spares and special tools at a price of $2,030,640 (US).
This price, which was negotiated by DDP through CCC, represents
the current cost of production J75 engines in the latest configuration less the cost of overhaul and installation of these
modifications required to bring the engines up to the latest
configuration. The cost to the Crown for these items was $8,568,000.
including spares and special tools. It is evident that by
buying prototypes and early production models we had to pay
for a portion of development and engineering costs. Had we been
able to wait for the later production, no doubt our bill would
have been much less.

3.   DDP have been negotiating with the U.S.A.F. for more
than a year and it seems that this is the best price they can
obtain.

4.   The attached submission seeks authority for the sale
and, also, for authority to place the proceeds in special account
for future purchase of materiel.

5.   No expenditure of public funds is involved.

6.   The submission can be approved under the authority
of Section 11 of the National Defence Act.

7.   The CAS recommends.

8.   I recommend.

L. M. Chesley
Assistant Deputy Minister

RCAF 1038CN/National Archives

*The Assistant Deputy Minister of National Defence briefs the Minister on the status of the J-75 sale back
to the USAF. All the groundwork has been laid. Everybody is in favour. The special account is referred to
and retained by DND for special procurement needs. I wonder if any other proceeds from the Arrow
programme cancellation ended up in RCAF's "special accounts."*

A memo outlining RCAF satisfaction with the deal and the so called "Special Account."

S202-6t(DAFB)
1038CN-60
Bor03
S202-H6/

MEMORANDUM

CR PA

21 Sep 60

DMP

Sale of J75 Engines to USAF

1   The submission to Treasury Board seeking authority for
the sale requested also that the proceeds should be credited to
Special Account for future purchase of materiel.

2   The Order in Council PC 1960-10/1249 dated 14 Sep
TB Minute 568997 approving, states that the proceeds may be used
for the procurement of defence materiel for the Canadian Forces.

3   The effect of this is satisfactory to the RCAF in that,
although it will not be credited directly to RCAF vote we can and
do, in the presentation of our Estimates state the amount standing
or expected to be to our credit in the Special Account and which
we propose to utilize, and this amount is deducted from our gross
cash requirement for expenditures to arrive at our net budgetary
cash figure.

4   Thus a substantial amount in our Special Account is of
considerable assistance to the RCAF in a tight or fixed budget year.

(EH Sharpe) G/C
DAFB
2-4074

P.S. I have assumed it is in
order for us to detach one copy
of CCC contract for our retention.

DMP

Please note

RCAF 1038CN/National Archives

CANADIAN COMMERCIAL CORPORATION
OTTAWA

DATE September 2, 1960.   CONTRACT

The Deputy Minister,
Department of National Defence,
125 Elgin Street,
Ottawa, Ontario.

ALL INVOICES, SHIPPING BILLS AND PACKING SLIPS
MUST SHOW THE FOLLOWING REFERENCE NUMBERS
CONTRACT NO. BX-16/7007-4-7
SERIAL NO.   7-BX-0-36
CONSIGNEE'S NO. AF33(600)-41745.

You are requested   to sell and/or supply to Canadian Commercial Corporation, upon the terms and
listed below and on any attached sheets or schedules   conditions set out herein and on the reverse side hereof, the supplies and/or services
below do not contain any amount representing   As the supplies are for export, you warrant that the price or prices set out
Duties paid upon the import of materials, parts and components incorporated or to be incorporated in the supplies.
Documentation as per attached Form(s)   CCC 162R6

ITEM	QUANTITY	DESCRIPTION OF SUPPLIES AND/OR SERVICES	Lot Price
1	15 each	J75-P-5PWA Engines suitable for economical overhaul and modification to J75-P-19W configuration.	XXXXX
2		J75 Engine Spars Parts, special tools, engine containers and YJ75-P-3 Spares Engines, to be selected by the U.S. Contracting Officer or his duly authorized representative from those available.	$2,030,640.00 U.S. Included in price of Item 1.

Item No.

Consignee

1   To - United Aircraft Corporation,
     Pratt & Whitney A/C Division,
     Air Parts Department,
     Southington, Connecticut.

2   Destinations to be specified at a
     later date as directed by this
     Corporation.

To be made within sixty (60) days after receipt of contract.

SHEET 1 OF 2   CASH DISCOUNT TERMS
                NET

ESTIMATED TOTAL AMOUNT
PAYABLE TO CONTRACTOR: $ 2,030,640.00 U.S.

FORM CCC 6 (8-1-59)

CANADIAN COMMERCIAL CORPORATION

PER

Here it is, the actual deed of sale which returns the engines to the USAF. You notice that the four J-75 P-3 engines are not on the list. What a lot of paperwork to get this sale through! Was everybody crossing their "t" and dotting their "i" just to be completely safe and beyond scrutiny?

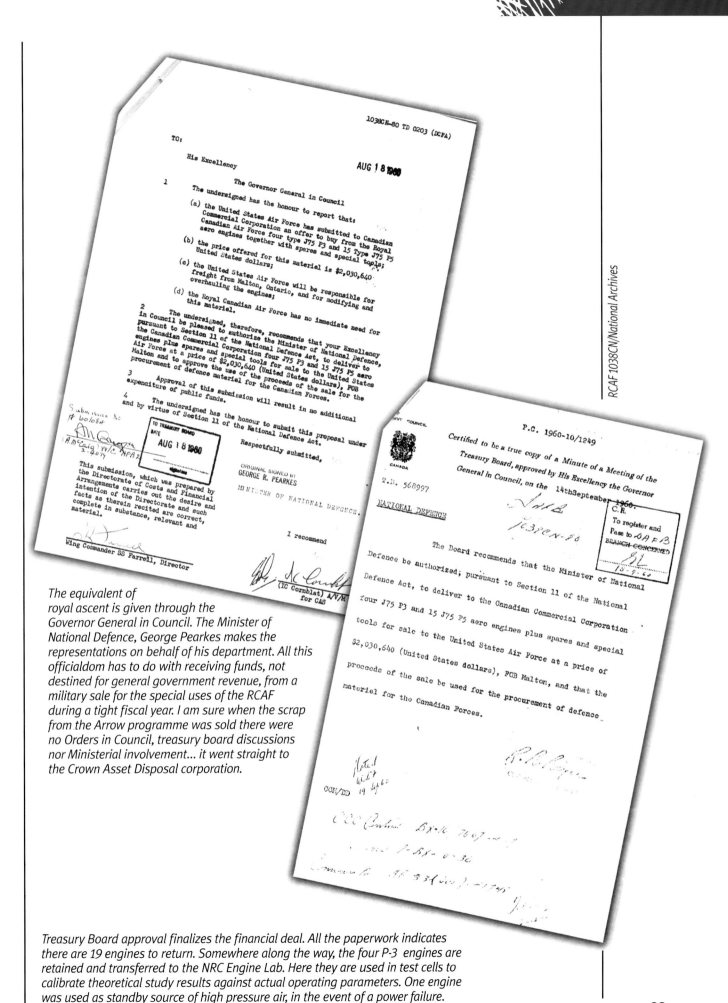

RCAF 1038CN/National Archives

The equivalent of royal ascent is given through the Governor General in Council. The Minister of National Defence, George Pearkes makes the representations on behalf of his department. All this officialdom has to do with receiving funds, not destined for general government revenue, from a military sale for the special uses of the RCAF during a tight fiscal year. I am sure when the scrap from the Arrow programme was sold there were no Orders in Council, treasury board discussions nor Ministerial involvement... it went straight to the Crown Asset Disposal corporation.

Treasury Board approval finalizes the financial deal. All the paperwork indicates there are 19 engines to return. Somewhere along the way, the four P-3 engines are retained and transferred to the NRC Engine Lab. Here they are used in test cells to calibrate theoretical study results against actual operating parameters. One engine was used as standby source of high pressure air, in the event of a power failure.

93

RCAF 1038CN/National Archives

Giving Arrow Technology Away...

UK Ministry of Supply asks for help in the development of their TSR2

IN REPLY PLEASE QUOTE
DRBC 0301-06

DEFENCE RESEARCH BOARD

DEPARTMENT OF NATIONAL DEFENCE
CANADA

Ottawa, Ontario.
27 July, 1959

Group Captain E.P. Bridgland,
CAE/DAEng,
Room 3068,
"B" Building,
National Defence Headquarters.

Arrow Reports

1.   In connection with the proposed development of the
TSR 2 aircraft, the Ministry of Supply has had a technical team
visiting Canada and the United States. The group discussed the
problems of high speed aircraft design with Avro Aircraft Ltd. as
well as a number of former Avro employees who held key positions
on the Arrow design team but who are now with Canadian and U.S.
research organizations, etc. During their visit the party ex-
pressed an interest in obtaining copies of the following reports:

1.	Elastic Longitudinal Derivatives	P/Aero/96
2.	Elastic Lateral Stability Derivatives	P/AD/97
3.	Lateral Dynamic Stability with improved tail stiffness	P/AD/89
4.	Damping System Development	P/Stability/137
5.	Structural Integrity Programme	71/FAR/34
6.	Arrow 2 Escape System	72/Eng Pub/2
7.	Specification for Escape System	
8.	Optimum Ejector Geometry for Arrow 2	P/Power/97
9.	Comparison of Theory and Experiment, J75 Inlet	P/Power/64
10.	Method for Calculation of Propulsion System Net Thrust	72/Int aero/6
11.	Revised Restrictor Geometry	72/Int aero/20
12.	Improvement of Subsonic Cruise, Arrow 2, by means of an Expendable Ejector Insert	72/Int aero/12
13.	Performance Characteristics of a Series of Divergent Shroud Ejectors	P/Power/95
14.	Theoretical Analysis of Optimum Ramp Angle for a Mach 2 Aircraft Incorporating the J75.	P/Power/48

2.   While some very minor effort may be needed to put
these reports in an acceptable form, Avro have indicated that it
should be possible to make copies available as required. Would
you please concur in the proposed transmission of the above-noted
documents to the Ministry of Supply for their use as required
during the development of the above-noted aircraft.

(H. C. Oatway)
Directorate of Engineering Research,
for Chairman, Defence Research Board.

Letter from the Defence Research Board to the RCAF, asking if the listed information may be shared with the UK Ministry of supply.

ANON

RCAF 1038CN/National Archives

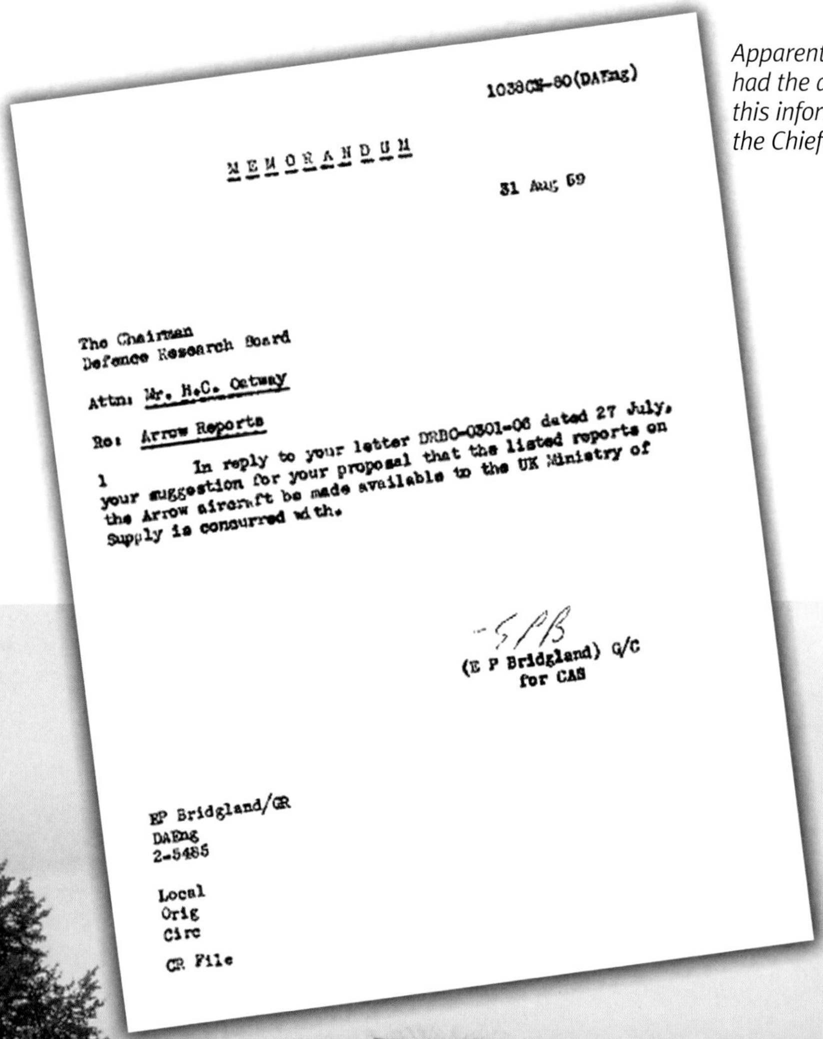

Apparently, Ed Bridgland had the authority to release this information on behalf of the Chief of the Air Staff.

1038CN-80(DAEng)

M E M O R A N D U M

31 Aug 69

The Chairman
Defence Research Board

Attn: Mr. H.C. Oatway

Re: Arrow Reports

1   In reply to your letter DRBC-0301-06 dated 27 July, your suggestion for your proposal that the listed reports on the Arrow aircraft be made available to the UK Ministry of Supply is concurred with.

(E P Bridgland) G/C
for CAS

EP Bridgland/GR
DAEng
2-5485

Local
Orig
Circ

CR File

At least the British kept 2 of their TSR2s. This one appears to be well weathered at Duxford, one of the RAF museums. Would the retention of one of our Arrows have diminished the current interest?

95

Arrow Countdown

More Wind-Tunnel Models Found at the NRC
Montreal Road, Ottawa

Although a lot of wind-tunnel work was done at The Cornell Aeronautical Laboratory in Buffalo, the National Research Council's fore-runner, the National Aeronautical Establishment did considerable work with high speed 1% models and low speed 7% models.

NRC//National Aeronautical Establishment

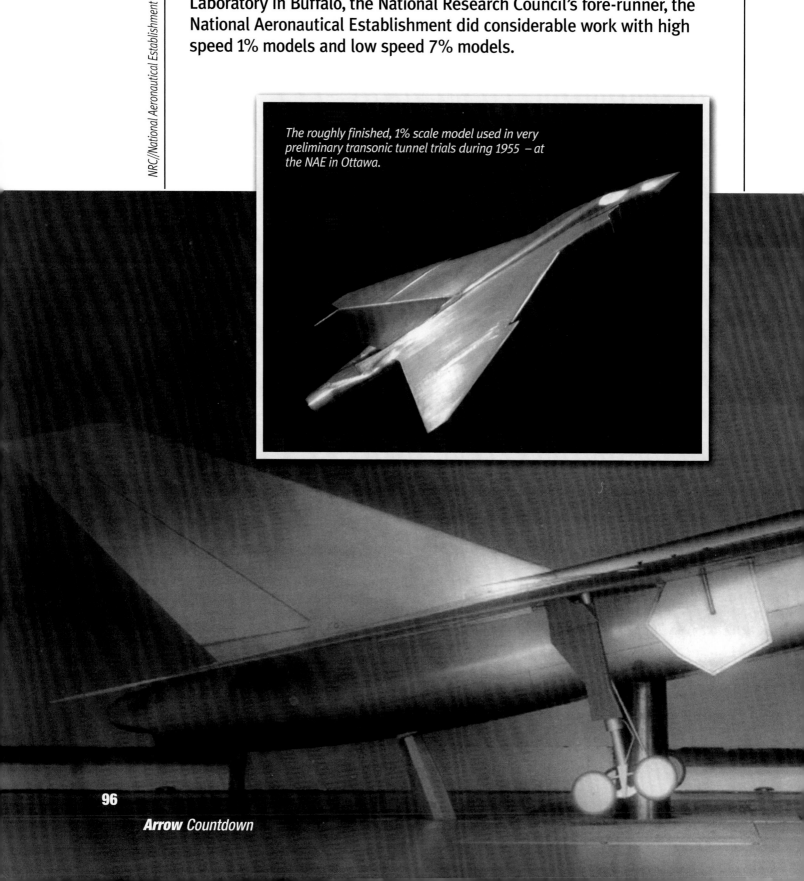

The roughly finished, 1% scale model used in very preliminary transonic tunnel trials during 1955 – at the NAE in Ottawa.

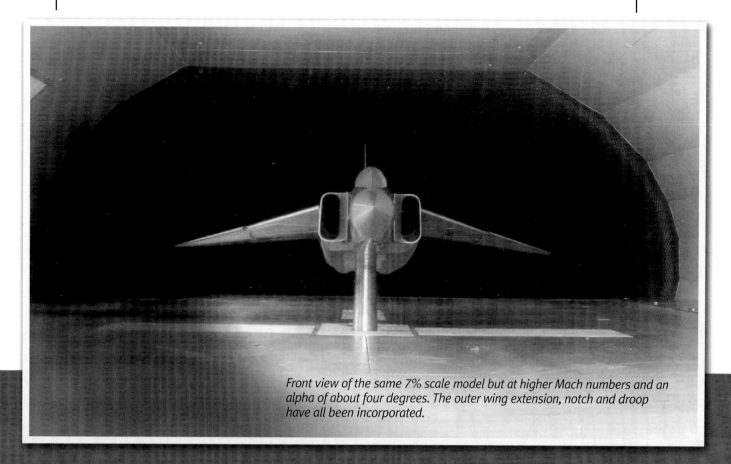

Front view of the same 7% scale model but at higher Mach numbers and an alpha of about four degrees. The outer wing extension, notch and droop have all been incorporated.

Seven percent scale Arrow model test on May 28, 1956, in the NAE's low speed wind tunnel (approximately MN 0.2-0.4). Landing trials at about 12 degree angle of attack are being explored. Note that the nose wheel retracted backwards in this model whereas in the final version the undercarriage retracted forward. The real enthusiast will further note the missing air duct entry shock plate boundary layer sucking venturi.

Iroquois Engine, X-116,
found in RAF Museum Storage shed

It was clear from the beginning that the engine, Iroquois X-116 was loaned , not given away, to Bristol Siddeley with the hope that they may find a use for the engine perhaps under a licence or a re-sale agreement. Of course, what they did is to take it apart, study it and incorporate the goodies found into the Olympus which was to power their TRS2 and later on the Concorde. After it had been studied, Rolls-Royce bought the company and consolidated the engine business in the UK. Cranfield College got the Iroquois in pieces and studied it further in their advanced jet engine development course. From there, it found its way to the RAF museum at Hendon, North of London. There was no room to

display it nor the expertise to put it back together again. It has languished in the R-100 dirigible hangers since the early nineties.

Its was always rumoured that an engine had found its way to the UK after the program. X-116 was easy, because at cancellation, it was orphaned at Avro and separated from the main batch of engines being rounded up and stored in the new High Altitude Test Facility at Orenda.

Marc-Andre Valiquette happened to be going to the UK on CAE business and to an airshow in the Hendon area. Naturally, in a lightening visit he found out that the engine was in the R100 storage facility and went and had a look. That's how we got these fantastic pictures, thanks to his timely and much appreciated efforts. The parts have been moved in 2001. We need to get them back before it is lost once again. The Alliance is spear-heading an initiative to do just that. We will keep you posted.

RCAF 1038CN/National Archives

Further memos, and confirmation, from the Department of Defence Production that the engine was LOANED.

RCAF 1038CN/National Archives

The striking-off the roll of the Iroquois engines at Orenda. Note X-116's absence!

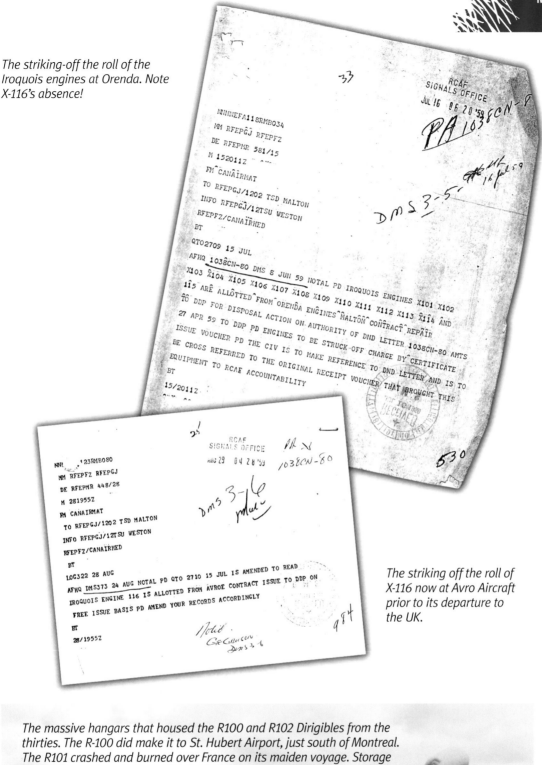

The striking off the roll of X-116 now at Avro Aircraft prior to its departure to the UK.

The massive hangars that housed the R100 and R102 Dirigibles from the thirties. The R-100 did make it to St. Hubert Airport, just south of Montreal. The R101 crashed and burned over France on its maiden voyage. Storage facility for our Orenda Iroquois!

Andre Valiquette

I kid you not... it is actually coincidence that the Iroquois should be displayed on pages 100 and 101... serendipity once again!

Andre Valiquette

The high speed, 8000 rpm plus, outer spool of X-116. Only one stage of the two stage high pressure turbine assemblies is attached. At the other end, the seven stages of the high pressure compressor rotor can be seen. The inner spool, with three stages of low compression and one stage of low pressure turbine is there, but not shown. Apparently all the guts and exterior parts are there!

The first fully variable thrust Iroquois afterburner sits majestically on its pallet.

Andre Valiquette

X-116's high pressure compressor outer casing is stacked on top of the engine inlet throat assembly. The front bearing assembly is just visible at the bottom of the stack. One of the unique weight-saving features of the Iroquois was the two bearing over-hung design. Engines of the day had at least three bearing assemblies.

Andre Valiquette

Andre Valiquette

Three more pallets with X-116 parts. The front pallet has the rear afterburner inlet assembly housing and afterburner jets and flame stabilizing gutters. The second pallet has the complete circular combustion chamber assembly. The last pallet has the outer magnesium casing of the low pressure compressor located between the inlet housing and the front bearing assembly.
Although we don't have pictures, I am assured that many other remaining parts, including a dolly, are all in storage at this facility.

101

CBC Mini-Series Model...

Alan Jackson started to build a near full-scale model of the Arrow in his garage – it ended up centre-stage in Winnipeg, co-starring, next to Dan Aykroyd in the 4-hour CBC mini-series, The Arrow.

Bill Zuk, a Winnipeg author and historian was there! He recorded in photo and text what happened during that summer in 1996. Here are some excerpts from that experience. Thank you Bill!

Bill Zuk

Bill Zuk

Alan Jackson tells his side of the Arrow story. He too, is recording the completion of his Arrow in the re-created world of the Fifties.

The mini-series featured a working model of the real aircraft. The origins of a scale model had an unusual beginning. It came from the workshop of Alan Jackson, a fifty-nine year old steel fabricator estimator working in Wetaskawin, AB. The passionate and dedicated Jackson had completed the nose section of the model by 1996. He envisioned completing the model by year 2000... the internet and The Arrow film producers changed that! Jackson had worked on the model based on plans found in the book "Avro Arrow" by the so-called Arrowheads. With the nose done, he next completed a wood and metal framework of the rest of the Arrow. When Jackson was approached to use the model in the movie, an arrangement was made to complete the model in Winnipeg, use it in the mini-series and then ship it back to him.

After the skeletal framework arrived in Winnipeg, it became the job of David Melrose, construction supervisor, to make it into the movie's Avro Arrow. The job had to be done in three weeks; ready to be featured in the outside shooting in June 1996. Melrose was faced with a daunting project. The replica had only to look like an Arrow. Movie-magic could make up for any short comings. With the need to get things done in a hurry, ten carpenters and craftsmen set down to work. The front view clearly shows the droop of the outer wings. It is not clear whether this was a design error, or if it was just too heavy to attach it and hang straight.

Bill Zuk

A sideview of the same movie Arrow before the fin is installed. To make the Arrow move for some of the action shots Melrose had devised a set of DC motors for each of the main gear wheels. One of the crew had the most "pilot" time by sitting in the navigator's compartment, controlling the motion through a hole in the floor... no forward view. This design feature was absent from the real Arrow. As it moved for the first time, the model shook off its dust and moved slowly ahead... it had come alive.

Bill Zuk

During August of 1996, model shooting of the radio controlled Arrow and CF-100 chase planes took place at Gimli on the shores of Lake Winnipeg. Not all flights were successful as can be seen by this crashed Arrow model. Doug Hislop of Calgary made the scale model and helped fly it from an accompanying helicopter. Takeoff was possible with a large bicycle wheeled platform... the model's small diameter landing gears created too much friction. Landings were tricky. A gust could flip it right over.

Bill Zuk

103

Bill Zuk

Dan Aykroyd as Crawford Gordon...
wouldn't it be great if he could attend
the real Arrow's roll-out once again...
but this time in Malton where it really
happened?

Alan Jackson Arrow...

Bill Zuk

RL 201

ELECTRONICS
ACCESS DOOR

There was no more important scene than the roll-out of
the movie's Arrow... once more on the centre stage of the
world. You will notice this carefully staged camera angle!
No sign of those droopy wings which sent shudders
through Arrow enthusiast's minds. When the crew was
finished with the Arrow they returned it to Alan Jackson in
Wetaskawin... but first they cut it up so that it could be
transported... can you believe it!

Rebuilding The Arrow

This completely detailed composite was painstakingly assembled by Joe Van Veenen. Fortunately, Avro designers used the same perspective angles, even though not all sketches were the same size. Stretching and twisting did the job. I think you will agree that it is the best internal detailed Arrow assembly seen yet. The source was the Arrow MKI Service Manual, fuselage section.

ALLIANCE **technical**

Avro's DC-3, piloted by Bill Devine, brought "Spud" and ground equipment to Trenton. It looks pretty cold!

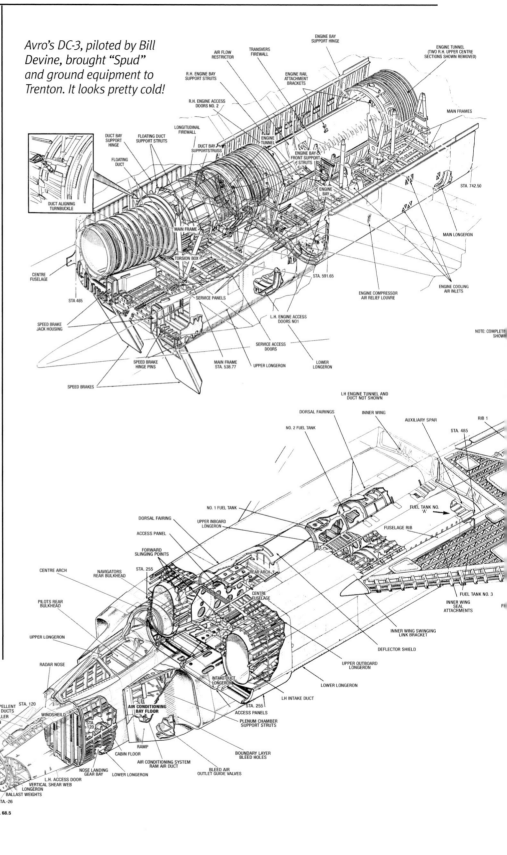

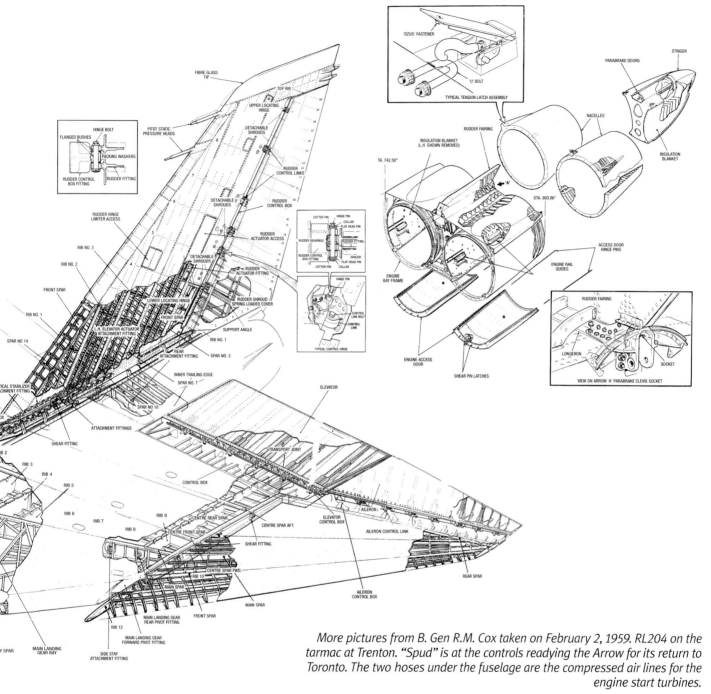

'DZUS' FASTENER

'U' BOLT

TYPICAL TENSION LATCH ASSEMBLY

STINGER

PARABRAKE DOORS

NACELLES

INSULATION BLANKET

RUDDER FAIRING

INSULATION BLANKET
(L.H. SHOWN REMOVED)

TA. 742.50"

STA. 803.06"

A

ENGINE BAY FRAME

ACCESS DOOR HINGE PINS

ENGINE RAIL GUIDES

ENGINE ACCESS DOOR

SHEAR PIN LATCHES

RUDDER FAIRING

LONGERON

SOCKET

VIEW ON ARROW 'A' PARABRAKE CLEVIS SOCKET

FIBRE GLASS TIP

TOP RIB

UPPER LOCATING HINGE

PITOT STATIC PRESSURE HEADS

DETACHABLE SHROUDS

HINGE BOLT

FLANGED BUSHES

PACKING WASHERS

RUDDER CONTROL BOX FITTING

RUDDER FITTING

RUDDER CONTROL LINKS

RUDDER CONTROL BOX

DETACHABLE SHROUDS

RUDDER HINGE LIMITER ACCESS

RIB NO. 3

RIB NO. 2

FRONT SPAR

RIB NO. 1

SPAR NO 14

RUDDER ACTUATOR ACCESS

DETACHABLE SHROUDS

RUDDER ACTUATOR FITTING

LOWER LOCATING HINGE

FRONT SPAR

RUDDER SHROUD SPRING LOADED COVER

L.H. ELEVATOR ACTUATOR ATTACHMENT FITTING

SUPPORT ANGLE

RIB NO. 1

REAR ATTACHMENT FITTING

SPAR NO. 3

INNER TRAILING EDGE

SPAR NO. 7

SPAR NO 10

COTTER PIN

HINGE PIN

COLLAR

FLAT HEAD PIN

RUDDER FITTING

RUDDER BEARINGS

RUDDER CONTROL BOX FITTING

SPACER

FLAT HEAD PIN

COTTER PIN

COLLAR

HINGE PIN

CONTROL LINK BOLT

CONTROL LINK

TYPICAL CONTROL HINGE

VERTICAL STABILIZER ATTACHMENT FITTING

E BOX

ATTACHMENT FITTINGS

SHEAR FITTING

RIB 2

RIB 3

RIB 4

RIB 5

RIB 6

RIB 7

RIB 8

RIB 9

RIB 10

MAIN SPAR

RIB 13

ELEVATOR

TRANSPORT JOINT

CONTROL BOX

CENTRE REAR SPAR

CENTRE SPAR AFT.

CENTRE FRONT SPAR.

CENTRE SPAR FWD.

SHEAR FITTING

ELEVATOR CONTROL BOX

AILERON

AILERON CONTROL LINK

AILERON CONTROL BOX

REAR SPAR

FRONT SPAR

MAIN SPAR

MAIN LANDING GEAR REAR PIVOT FITTING

MAIN LANDING GEAR FORWARD PIVOT FITTING

SIDE STAY ATTACHMENT FITTING

ARY SPAR

MAIN LANDING GEAR BAY

More pictures from B. Gen R.M. Cox taken on February 2, 1959. RL204 on the tarmac at Trenton. "Spud" is at the controls readying the Arrow for its return to Toronto. The two hoses under the fuselage are the compressed air lines for the engine start turbines.

RL 204

25204

We know, in detail, what the Arrow looked like!

AVRO Brochure MKII "Arrow Performance"

An artist's impression of Arrows on patrol. The sleek aircraft looks as modern today as it did then... back in the fifties. It is interesting to note that the new mission of the RCAF may be to fly high and fast as opposed to low and manoeuverable. Maybe there is room for the Arrow yet?

Why rebuild the Arrow?

In the fifties, the Arrow was a symbol of technical competence and a source of National pride. It raised aspirations of a generation. Even today, many Canadians can point to a relative or friend who was somehow connected to the project. A rebuilt Arrow can bring closure for those who were there – many are still alive. We can inspire a new generation to set their goals at an elevated level, achieve them and feel a great sense of accomplishment.

I thought everything was destroyed!

The Alliance has uncovered hundreds of technical manuals, drawings and plans. Many wind tunnel models and data have been found. About 45% of the Arrow has been recovered along with 7 engines from the program, four J-75s and three Iroquois. An Arrow Technical Advisory Council has been formed. It is made up of aviation industry experts from many different quarters, schools and corporations. It is a fluid group whose job is, to advise on the methodology and details required to rebuild an airworthy Arrow. There are thousands of Canadian Aerospace workers in Canada. We are third in the world in the field of commercial aviation. We really do have something to celebrate.

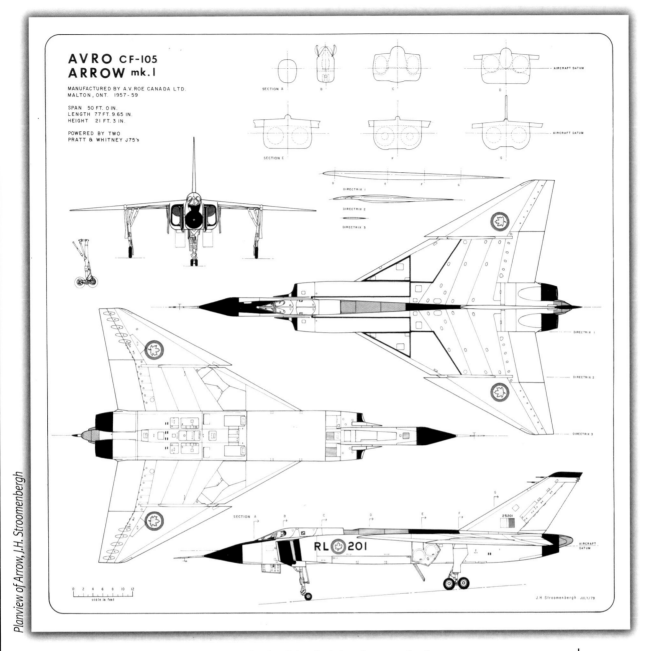

AVRO CF-105
ARROW mk.1

MANUFACTURED BY A.V.ROE CANADA LTD.
MALTON, ONT. 1957-59

SPAN 50 FT. 0 IN.
LENGTH 77 FT. 9.65 IN.
HEIGHT 21 FT. 3 IN.

POWERED BY TWO
PRATT & WHITNEY J75's

Planview of Arrow, J.H. Stroomenbergh

*Traditional drafting views of the Arrow. Hundreds of detailed drawings survived.
There are many more to find.*

How can we rebuild the Arrow?

The Alliance will use the same proven techniques that have made Canadian aviation what it is today. New tools such as computer modeling/design, CNC machining and laser cutting will reduce traditional hard steel work. Using the same trial phases of wooden mock-up, metal mock-up and final build ensures it all comes together in the end. Remote manufacture, so successful today, can be included in the Arrow rebuild. Parts could be assembled in the old facility at Malton, which still exists, using a small skeleton staff of specialists, hired to do the job. A first flight corridor is still in use at Malton. The military has toyed with the idea of handling taxi and first flight logistics/execution. We can do it!

Veridian Engineering Report

Wind Tunnel Data and Arrow Model Drawings Recovered in Buffalo

In the nineteen fifties the Cornell Aeronautical Laboratory, situated in Buffalo, New York , was contracted to carry out extensive wind-tunnel work in their continuous transonic facility. When the programme was cancelled the RCMP came down to destroy any work remaining at the plant. A smart employee loaded the back of a van with what he could carry, took it over to Fort Erie for the day, and went back after they had gone. This way 91 drawings of the Arrow wind tunnel models were saved as well as bundles of test results, primarily of the 4% scale Arrow model now in the possession of Ken Barnes, Etobicoke. The Alliance has entertained the thought of sprucing up this model and getting it into the Mach 4 tunnel at Uplands, Ottawa. New techniques of measuring pressure profiles that are non-invasive, using pressure sensitive paint can shed more refined light on the Arrow wings. As it is, Richard Poole, a retired Dehaviland aerodynamicist, took the three inch thick tabulation of wind tunnel results and used them to plot a new set of parameters, one of which is shown.

Cornell Aeronautical Laboratory Wind-tunnel was used extensively by Avro to determine optimal shape for minimal drag. It still operates today under Veridian Engineering. A long-term aero industry asset.

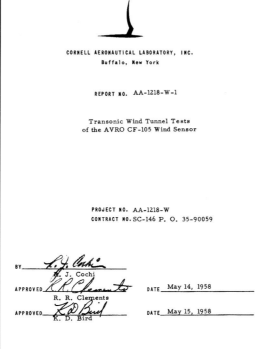

Cornell Aeronautical Lab Report

The last Avro study at Cornell verified the operation and drag effects of the long data boom which extended forward from the Arrow's radome.

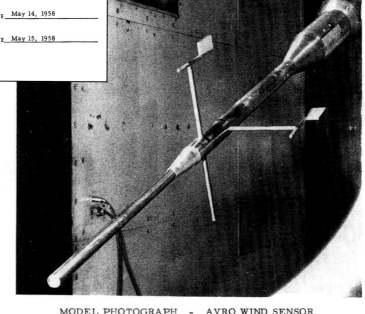

MODEL PHOTOGRAPH - AVRO WIND SENSOR

Cornell Aeronautical Lab Report

The Arrow data boom with alpha and beta vanes attached. Alpha was pitch and beta was side-slip. Relative wind sensors made flying the Arrow easier. A new, still in the crate, boom is stored at the National Aviation Museum in Ottawa.

Cornell labs retained a lot of the Arrow files. All wind tunnel results are still there and copied for our use. Ninety-one drawings of the Arrow were still in the vault and given to the Alliance to help in the rebuild.

Richard Poole

Veridian Exit Permission, Buffalo, New York

FM-1.2.02-SOF-041-R02

VERIDIAN

No. 12796

P.O. Box 400, 4455 Genesee Street, Buffalo, NY 14225
(716) 632-7500

SHIPPING ORDER FORM

SHIP TO:		HAZARDOUS MATERIAL
Company Peter Zuuring		Yes ☐ No ☒

Address (P.O. Box unacceptable unless sent through U.S. Mail) 21570 The Laggan Rd., RR #1 Dalkeith	Phone No. 613-874-2838

City, State Ontario, Canada	Zip Code K0B 1E0	A/B or B/L #

Attention	Required Arrival Date: AM ☐ PM ☐	

SHIPPING LABELS ARE REQUIRED	**Customer Deliverable** Yes ☐ No ☐	No. of Containers
Ship via: Hand Carry Out of Veridian Engineering		Size
Prepaid ☐ Collect ☐	Value $	**On Time** Yes ☐ No ☐	Weight

Dated Issued	Insure $	Inspection Required	Packed by Date

Date Shipped	Project		*LABEL NEEDED*
	Account		

REASON ☐ Sale ☒ Loan ☐ Repair ☐ Reject ☐ Replacement	Miscellaneous and/or Remark:
☐ Credit ☐ Relief of Accountability ☐ Consignment	

Purchase Order No.	Customer P.O. or Reference

Item No.	Quantity	Unit	Description	Location
1	1	Lot	CF 105 AVRO Aero Drawings - See Attached List	

Requested By Joyce O.	Authorized By Doug Stryker
Org. Abbrev. TWT	Tel. 5126	Org. Abbrev. TWT	Tel. 6882

Page 1 of 1

AVRO Photo

Arrow master models on display. These will have to be recreated to confirm the exterior shape of the Arrow much as was done in the fifties. The Arrow was defined from the outside to the inside. Usually, it was done the other way around.

111

The Canadian Aeronautical Journal, the official publication of the Canadian Aeronautical Institute was, and still is, a tremendous source of Arrow technology. During the fifties Avro/Orenda engineers and executives often contributed major articles describing events at Malton and their baby the Arrow.

Canadian Aeronautical Journal

CAI Logo

Arrow MKI centre sections fill the southern half of bay one. The amount of detail in these glossy 8 X10 B/W photos is amazing... a good source of info on manufacturing methods. There were five MK I Arrows. Arrow 201 can be seen at the top of the photo with the other four sections lined up towards it.

AVRO Photo

The rubber press, largest in the world at this time stretched nearly two stories underground. A large hydraulic system pressed the working table up into the more than one foot thick rubber pad. Aluminum cutouts would take the shape of the form under it as the rubber pressed down around it. This press is still operating today in the old plant now owned by Boeing. Great service life.

TOOLING APPROACH TO ARROW AIRCRAFT†

by E. B. Bragg*

Avro Aircraft Limited

THE Arrow is an extremely high performance aircraft necessitating a high degree of envelope accuracy and surface smoothness to achieve the required aerodynamic efficiency. For this reason, Avro management established a basic policy which governs the whole engineering and manufacturing approach to production. Irksome though this may have seemed at times to both Engineering and Production, it was felt that this policy was mandatory to effect the requirements of the Royal Canadian Air Force and the Department of Defence Production in producing the best possible product for the purpose intended.

An important part of this policy was that production tooling would be provided for an agreed production rate from the first aircraft. The reasons here are obvious, since such a highly complex piece of equipment requires a degree of tooling sufficient to ensure the product quality in itself, regardless of quantity, and also that a prototype program requiring extensive tooling readjustment for production would involve a prohibitive addition to the flow time.

In order to minimize design changes and possible production bottlenecks, close liaison was established with Production Engineering people situated in the Engineering Department. One of the first problems that had to be tackled was engineering release to production. An agreed breakdown and release schedule was essential so that planning, tooling and production could produce the right parts for the successive assembly stages in their proper sequence.

There is an element of risk in starting on an intensive tooling program concurrent with early product design effort. However, since the spectre of early obsolescence looms over all such products in such a rapidly developing sphere of science, it is essential to use all reasonable means to shorten flow times.

In order that a vehicle having maximum serviceability be provided, it was mandatory that from the first airplane a high degree of interchangeability should be maintained. Accordingly, Avro Production Engineering Department, in collaboration with the RCAF Design Engineering and Inspection Department, established the interchangeability of components and parts. An "Interchangeability Tooling Program" which would control the requisite points in their relative positions on the assembly fixtures was therefore mandatory, and, moreover,

†Paper read at the Annual General Meeting of the C.A.I. on the 27th May, 1958, in Toronto.
*Production Engineering Manager.

362

Canadian Aeronautical Journal

Figure 1
Component breakdown

Figure 2
Outline of centre fuselage

CAI Article, Journal

A classic article from the Journal discussing the tooling approach to Arrow production. Detailed discussions describe the whole procedure from design through final assembly. A bulkhead example from the centre section is followed through the whole process. Pictures illustrate and illuminate. Although CNC milling and laser cutting are new today, many old tried and true methods still apply.

Industry Documents Complement Avro's Extensive Photo Record

It is amazing to me that a supposedly 'Secret' project was well written up by industry publications and professional organizations. Everywhere, during the fifties, there was talk of and information on the Arrow. Even Jim Floyd, former V.P. of Engineering at Avro, gave an extensive talk on the whole Arrow story, from beginning to its current development , to the British Royal Aeronautical Society meeting in London, December 1958. Many other Avro executives spoke on the development, manufacture and operation of the Arrow. The Alliance is slowly gathering this treasure trove and will be using it to good effect.

Photos continue to surface. I have to especially thank Earle Brownridge's son, Glen, for providing a substantial cache on the Orenda/Iroquois front. Lou Wise, Avro head of photography, is still around. He says he has nothing but who knows! Hundreds of good quality photos have now surfaced. Have you got more? Get in touch with the Alliance!

Another milestone article from the Journal. The machining approach to Arrow production parts is fully illustrated with accompanying photos. Spars, special joints, go, no-go jigs and more. Working special grades of aluminum was a learning process. How much stretch forming to reduce machining stresses? What type of heat treating, quenching etc., etc. Another great reference text.

The Avro autoclave is also still functioning at the, now Boeing, Malton facility. Aluminum/magnesium sheets were bonded under heat and pressure to form new light weight composite panels for the skin of the Arrow. Again the technology has not changed a great deal, although there are many so called "space-age composites" than ever before. However, airplanes are still made in much the same way as they were in the fifties.

CAI Journal

MACHINING APPROACH TO AIRCRAFT PRODUCTION

by H. F. Young*

Avro Aircraft Limited

In this paper on the machining approach to aircraft production, I propose to present some of the problems encountered on our latest program and the action taken to prepare ourselves for this relatively new type of manufacturing.

MATERIALS

Very early in the design stages, our Engineers determined that integrally stiffened skins and completely machined structural members were necessary to meet the design requirements. From this overall requirement, the first essential to be settled was the choice of materials. We decided to use the experience gained in the United Kingdom and the United States and machine from rolled plate and solid billets.

In reviewing some of our exceptional problems in these fields, I propose to disregard conventional materials, such as extrusions, castings and bar stock, that we have used on previous programs and will continue to use.

Stretcher stress relieved plate

We were advised by companies using heavy plate that this material should be stretcher stress relieved to minimize distortion during machining. Figure 1 shows the advantages of using material in this condition. The skin on the left-hand side was made from stretcher stress relieved plate and has no appreciable bow, while the skin on the right-hand side was made from standard rolled stock; the advantages of stress relieving are very apparent. The degree of stretch needed is illustrated in Figure 2. To obtain the maximum flatness of plate, a stretch of 0.5%, is sufficient but, to stress relieve the plate, 2.0%, is required to provide a permanent set.

The size of stretcher level plate available on the commercial market at the present time is limited to the capacity of the machine shown in Figure 3, which has a maximum pull of 6,000,000 lb and is capable of stretching a cross-sectional area of 140 sq in. Though not clearly shown in this figure, the hydraulic jaws will handle a 3" thick plate.

It is understood that the suppliers of plate are investigating the possibility of doubling the cross-sectional area and thickness I have quoted in the very near future.

†Paper read at the Annual General Meeting of the C.A.I. in Montreal on the 3rd May, 1956.
*Chief Production Engineer

252

Figure 1
Comparison of skins made from stretcher stress relieved plate, left, and rolled stock, right

Figure 2
The effects of increased percentage stretch

Canadian Aeronautical Journal

AVRO Photo

There were six milled skin panels, left and right, top and bottom on each inner wing of the Arrow. Thousands of pounds of scrap aluminum were created by reducing large heavy billets of hundreds of pounds to thin contoured, with integrally machined stiffeners, skin panels. The skin mill shown was state of the art for the day and the biggest ever installed. It is no longer in service. John Connell operated this mill & is seen inspecting one of the Arrow inner wing skins.

AVRO Photo, John Connell

113

Many reference materials have survived

AVRO Photo

The flight controls system test bed found that there were differences from the command settings called for and the actual control position obtained. Hangups in the control cables stiffened the response. This type of testing system will have to be repeated for the rebuild programme of the new Arrow.

The electrical system, air conditioning controls and landing gear servos were tested through this mock-up. Behind the panel, the test rig stretched for 30 feet incorporating all the cable runs, terminal boxes and electrical components.

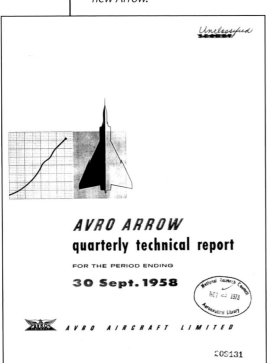

Unclassified
~~SECRET~~

AVRO ARROW
quarterly technical report

FOR THE PERIOD ENDING

30 Sept. 1958

National Research Council
OCT 25 1973
Aeronautical Library

AVRO AIRCRAFT LIMITED

209131

AVRO Report

The Alliance has found five Quarterly Technical Reports through '57 and '58. These have proven to be invaluable. The detail design changes, the research that went into it, and the solutions found, these are key to making sure that the latest thoughts and modifications are incorporated into the rebuild.

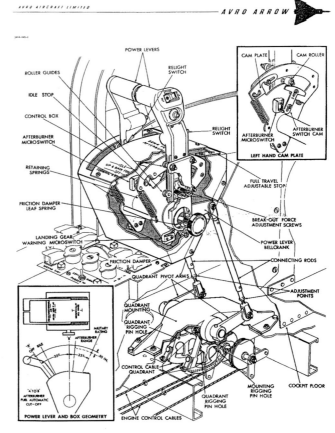

FIG. 30 POWER CONTROL BOX AND LINKAGE

In a quarterly Technical Review, the work done on the cockpit throttle assembly is detailed. Apparently, there was spring-back in the cable system to the actuator located at the engine itself. The cable tensioners at the throttle had to be redesigned to accommodate. Detailed drawings with explanations make up the modification. Note that the cables do not pass through the floor of the cockpit. It was pressurized so they had to be connected by a sealed crank arrangement.

Former Avro Employees have retained important information

Once aerodynamic information has described the shape of the plane, structure, loading and stress engineers go about the task of determining the interior materials, shape and thickness of the aircraft. Hank Shoji headed up Avro's stress group. His family donated all his notes, quality control manuals, area rule studies and more.

Ross Richardson designed the intakes and front fuselage of the Arrow. He has all his original work on the crucial intake design.

Doug Moore was in charge of the Arrow's centre section. He is alive and has a fantastic memory. He amply showed me as we crawled and poked around RL206 in the Ottawa National Aviation Museum.

Bob Cairns wrote the specifications of the Arrow. He has donated copies of the January 1959 latest updates as well as detailed specifications on RL206, 7, 8, and 9, the first real Arrow MK II production version.

Many have come forward... will you?

Shoji Family

Hank's findings are detailed in many of the reports his family donated to the Alliance for the rebuild. This is the cover of one of them.

THE HYDRAULIC PIPE PROBLEM WITH PARTICULAR
REFERENCE TO THE 4,000 P.S.I. SYSTEM

H.N. Shoji.

AVRO AIRCRAFT LIMITED
MALTON, ONTARIO
CANADA

Date: November, 1958.

Hank Shoji was head of the stress group designing the fin of the Arrow. He was involved with many different stress related problems requiring fatigue testing... not the least of which was the ins and outs of operating a 4,000 psi hydraulic system. His family has been very helpful in providing original engineering manuals and many design notes on the torsion box design of the Arrow wing. Thank you!

This is the test rig for cycling 4,000 psi fittings, pipe joints, bends and junctions to see the effect of butt joining versus swageing on the integrity of a hydraulic pipe run. Butt joints worked better. Off the shelf 3,000 psi hydraulic systems are the norm today. For the rebuild we will still have to go to the 4,000 psi level for the same reason as then... namely, to make powerful actuators small enough to fit into the thin wings.

AVRO Photo

Fatigue testing through stress bending and cycling was well developed at Avro. In the foreground is the wing box test stand with a box in place undergoing tests. Strain gauges measure defections to ultimate failure. In the background you can see the engine bay formers, cut out of whole billets, assembled and put through cyclical fatigue testing. Because the Arrow would pass through the sound barrier often more long life flexibility was the required norm.

115

Boeing Staff Photographer

The first ATAC, Arrow Technical Advisory Council, meets at the old Avro Malton facility, in the engineering training room on the second floor at the end of Bay #1.
A disrupting snow storm caused some members to leave early. The group that remained are:
Seated front row; David McMillan, Pro Engineering design, Peter Zuuring, Founder of the Alliance, Al Ludford, RCAF pilot retired, Richard Poole, Aerodynamicist retired Dehaviland,
Back row; Alex Tsulus, Boeing Loading and Stress engineer
Jeff Brownridge, grandson of Earle, Mohawk College student, Francis Lau, Stress engineer, Bombardier Richard Nakka, Bombardier and Kevin Bruce from Transport Canada.
Early departure; Paul Hayes, Canadian Forces advisor, Absent; Steve Shaw, Shaw Productions, Ernie Burnett, AVRO Weight and Balance, Ken Hitchnough, NRC/IRAP representative, Bruce Yarmashita, Dowty

The 'Arrow Technical Advisory Council' meets as a First Step

On a snowy day, March 15, 2001 the *ad hoc* members of ATAC meet at the old Avro Malton plant. Not everyone who had agreed to come, makes it because of the weather. Nonetheless, we kick-off and have a good meeting. The overall purpose of the meeting was to sound out from experts in the aviation field what they thought of rebuilding a flying Arrow. We got it in spades!

After an introduction of what the Alliance was trying to accomplish, each representative spoke.

Generally, the task was described as daunting. There was concern over funding. The need for a core group of specialists that would stay with the project was emphasized. The flight envelope should be conservative. A mach 2.0 aircraft would cost much more to recreate than one that just broke the sound barrier to create the boom, say mach 1.2. Concerns were raised about adequate testing of components and assemblies. Transport Canada raised the issue of flight control software. This is a new area. The work done on the Bombardier's Global Express might be of interest. This is currently a difficult part of aircraft certification. An interesting comment was when the weight of your documentation equals the weight of your aircraft you are probably ready. The Alliance was encouraged to get our story out to the aviation industry and to solicit their support early on. Time is of the essence.

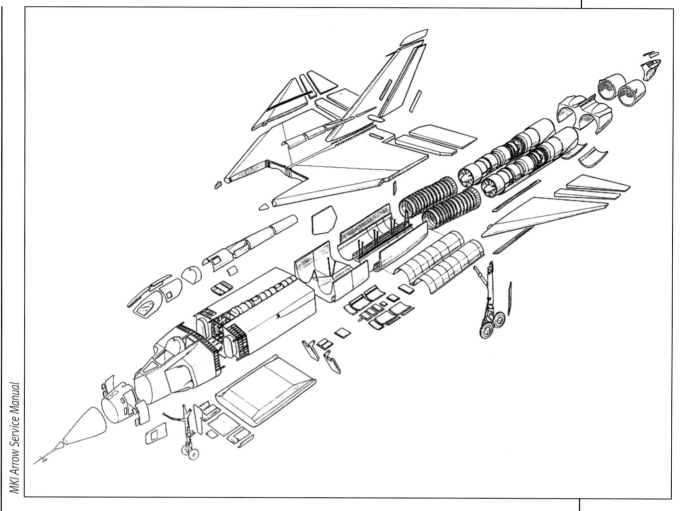

MKI Arrow Service Manual

Component breakdown of the Arrow. There is no reason to change this configuration for the rebuild. It worked then and should do fine now. Various aircraft manufacturers can build these to our specifications, be gathered together in Malton and re-assembled into the finished Arrow.

Getting the military involved made sense to everyone: even though they have no money, they have expertise. According to one member, the talent at Cold Lake is depleting and we should get to them quickly.

I was pleased about the mention of Cold Lake. Last year, I was the guest of honour at the Annual Mess Dinner. I was asked to stay a few days after and had the opportunity to really check out the CF18 aircraft generally, the extensive installations and support facilities. On the last day, the access panels were removed from one of the CF18s and I had a good look under the skin, so to speak. I was amazed to find very similar system components to

those on the Arrow. The same suppliers are still in business – we should be able to buy off the shelf complete hydraulic, air conditioning, fuel, oxygen, electrical systems just to name a few. It reduces our job to building a first-rate airframe, adding off the shelf component systems and fitting a suitable Iroquois replacement such as the Pratt & Whitney F-100. This engine is of the right weight to thrust ratio of the Iroquois, is available, proven, maintainable and safe.

In general the meeting was cautiously optimistic/enthusiastic. All left the meeting somewhat excited... now we have to get on with it!

Irvin is located in Fort Erie, Ontario. They made chutes for the Arrow. They can do it again!

AVRO Photo

technical BULLETIN
Arrow

VOLUME ONE

NUMBER ONE

SPECIAL BOOK ISSUE

RL205 One and only landing, AVRO

Arrow Parabrake

Arrow Parabrake

GENERAL

1 A parachute brake is fitted in the rear fuselage stinger, between the engine nacelles aft of the rudder.

2 The parachute is streamed on touchdown to assist in reducing the aircraft landing run and to prolong the life of the aircraft wheels and brakes. The complete parachute assembly can be jettisoned by the pilot when the landing run is complete.

3 The parachute brake assembly consists of a selector lever, control cable, cable tension regulator, parabrake box, door release mechanism, parabrake release mechanism and a parachute assembly.

4 The selector lever is mounted in a quadrant outboard of the power levers. The knob of the lever is shaped like a parachute for easy identification. A plate marked STREAM and JETTISON with arrows to indicate the selector lever movement is riveted to the quadrant. Selection of STREAM is accomplished by moving the lever downwards to a gate position. The lever is prevented from springing back to the doors closed position by a spring-loaded lock plate.

Selection of JETTISON is accomplished by an inward and downward movement from the STREAM position. To reset the selector lever to the doors closed position it is necessary to release the lock plate.

CONTROL CABLE

5 A 3/32 inch steel cable runs from the selector lever and tension regulator in the cockpit to the release mechanism in the rear fuselage. The cable runs through the front fuselage, armament bay and rear fuselage, over pulleys and through fairleads, to a spring damper in the release mechanism. The control cable shares pulley banks with the flying control cables at stations 280 and 485. A turnbuckle is provided in the armament bay to connect and adjust the control cable.

6 A cable tension regulator, connected to the selector lever quadrant by a short input cable, is fitted on the cockpit floor. It is sealed to prevent leakage of cabin pressure. The regulator maintains a tension on the output cable under all conditions of temperature and structural flexing. When tension is applied to the input cable, a clutch in the tension regulator locks the input and output cables to give a positive pull through the regulator.

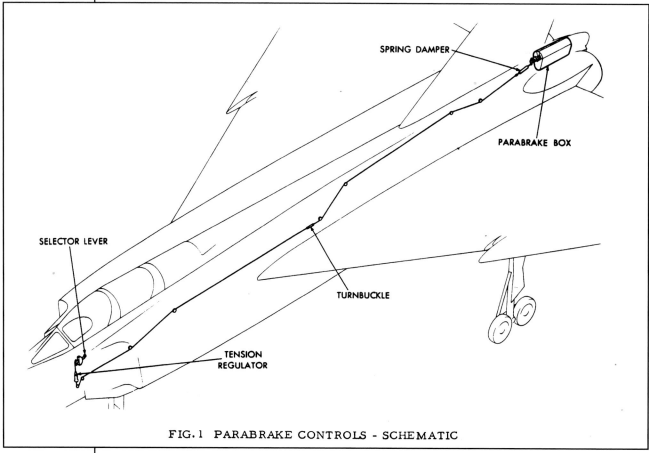

FIG. 1 PARABRAKE CONTROLS - SCHEMATIC

SELECTOR LEVER (Fig 1)

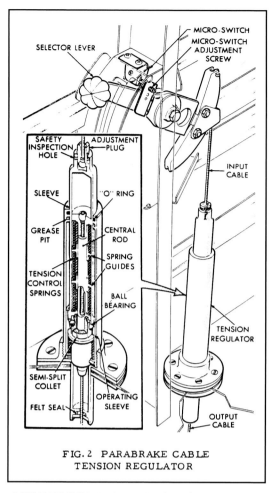

FIG. 2 PARABRAKE CABLE
TENSION REGULATOR

CABLE TENSION REGULATOR (Fig 2)

7 The clutch consists of a central rod, a semi-split collect, eight ball bearings and a sleeve. The central rod is attached to the output cable and moves with the cable. The input cable is attached to the sleeve. The semisplit collect fits over the central rod and has eight segments with a tapered flute machined on each. Attached to the lower end of the sleeve, is an operating sleeve with eight matching tapered flutes machined on its inner surface. A ball bearing is inserted in the space between each flute of the operating sleeve and the semisplit collect.

8 When tension is applied to the input cable, it pulls upwards on the sleeve and the ball bearings force the segments of the semisplit collect against the central rod. The central rod then transfers the load to the output cable.

9 When tension on the input cable is relieved, tension control springs push the sleeve downwards against a stop. A spring fitted under the clutch then pushes the semi-split collect upwards to disengage the clutch.

10 With no load on the input cable, the tension control springs maintain a tension of 25 lbs. on the output cable when they are fully compressed, and a tension of 8.5 lbs. when they are fully extended.

The circle clearly indicates the Parabrakeing Chute control lever placement on the left side of the cockpit. "Spud" Potocki strongly counseled would-be Arrow pilots to be able to reach for it without looking. The lever was up during flight. One pull down to the stop streamed the chute. The detent was overcome by pulling out and down to detach the chute at the end of the breaking roll. The knob at the end of the lever was shaped in the form of an open chute.

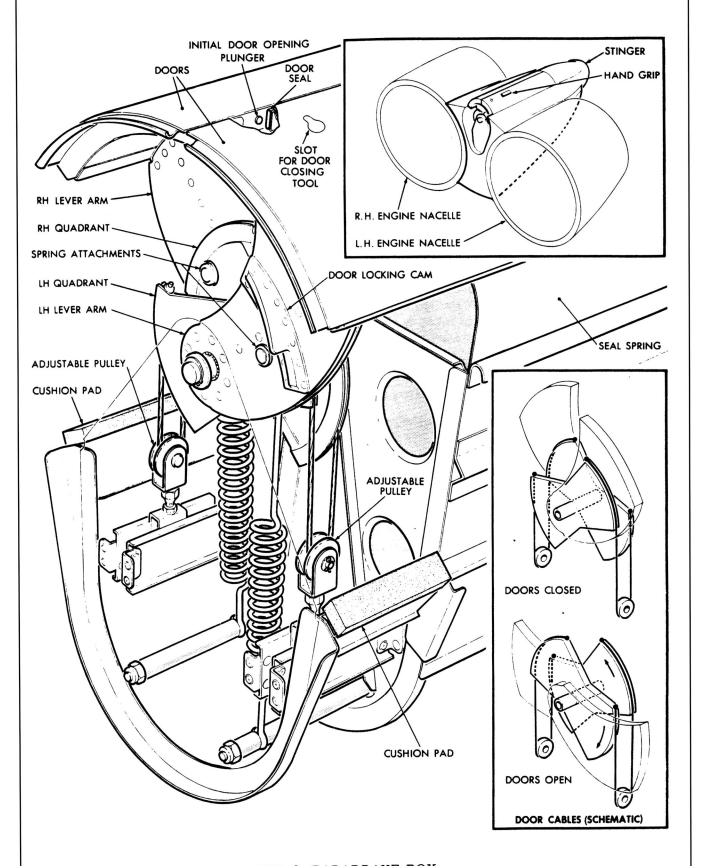

INITIAL DOOR OPENING PLUNGER

DOORS

DOOR SEAL

SLOT FOR DOOR CLOSING TOOL

RH LEVER ARM

RH QUADRANT

SPRING ATTACHMENTS

LH QUADRANT

LH LEVER ARM

ADJUSTABLE PULLEY

CUSHION PAD

DOOR LOCKING CAM

STINGER

HAND GRIP

R.H. ENGINE NACELLE

L.H. ENGINE NACELLE

SEAL SPRING

ADJUSTABLE PULLEY

CUSHION PAD

DOORS CLOSED

DOORS OPEN

DOOR CABLES (SCHEMATIC)

FIG. 3 PARABRAKE BOX

PARABRAKE BOX (Fig 3)

11 A parabrake box located in the fuselage stinger between the engine nacelles provides stowage for the parachute assembly. The upper-section of the box is enclosed by two curved doors pivoted on lever arms at each end. Quadrants riveted to the two forward lever arms are connected together by two wire cables running over two adjustable pulleys. This synchronizes the operation of the doors, and provides positive locking of both doors when the LH door is locked. A cam on the LH forward lever arm engages with a spring-loaded cam follower to lock the doors in the closed position. When the cam follower is withdrawn by the selector lever, the doors are opened by two coil springs attached to the lever arms. An initial opening spring, fitted at the forward end of the RH door between the inner and outer door skins provides an assist to the initial opening movement. In the open position, the doors rest on four rubber cushion pads. A handgrip is provided on the inner and outer skin of each door to facilitate manual closing. A keyhole slot in the LH door provides a means of fitting a door closing tool.

12 A small hinged door, secured by quick release fasteners, is fitted in the RH door to provide access to the pin and bracket to which the pilot chute release pin is attached after the doors are closed.

PARABRAKE INDICATOR

13 An indicator fitted in the parabrake box gives an external indication that the parachute assembly is installed, without the necessity of opening the parabrake doors. The indicator consists of a spring-loaded platform connected to an indicator rod sliding in a guide tube. The spring-loaded platform is hinged to the lower skin of the parabrake box, and when the parachute assembly is removed, the platform rises and the indicator rod protrudes through a hole in the lower skin of the rear fuselage stinger. When the parachute assembly is installed, the platform is held down and the indicator rod is withdrawn into the guide tube.

DOOR RELEASE MECHANISM (Fig 4)

14 A parabrake box door release mechanism is fitted in the upper section of the rear fuselage at station 803. It consists of a spring damper, an actuating lever with linkage, and a ca follower. Movement of the selector lever to STREAM moves the spring damper rod forward and operates the actuating lever, pulling the cam follower out of engagement with the parabrake door cam. Two coil springs attached to the forward lever arms and to the box structure open the two doors when the lock

AVRO Photo

Ian Higgins and Pete Bonell worked in flight test. One of their duties was to collect a spent chute from the runway and repack it for use once again. In the small rectangular building on the west side of the flight test flight line, Ian Higgins has laid out a chute for refolding and packing. Check out the 30+ foot long, narrow, table.

is released. When the doors are closed, the spring-loaded cam follower engages with the cam on the LH door lever arm and locks the doors in this position. The selector lever must be in the doors closed position and the master electrical switch must be OFF before closing the doors.

ELECTRICAL SAFETY LOCK (Figs 2 and 4)

15 A solenoid operated safety lock in the release mechanism prevents inadvertent opening of the parabrake box doors. When the selector lever is in the doors closed position a microswitch on the selector lever energizes the solenoid. The solenoid plunger retracts and actuates a locking lever to lock the cam follower in the extended position. Initial movement of the selector lever opens the micro-switch and de-energizes the solenoid. In the event of electrical failure the lock is in the released position.

ELECTRICAL SAFETY LOCK INDICATOR LIGHT

16 An indicator light, located on the refuel and test panel forward of the LH speed brake and marked PARABRAKE LOCK, is illuminated by a relay when the electrical safety lock solenoid plunger is retracted. The indicator light provides an indication that the cam follower is extended and the lock is engaged. The indi cator light is a "press -to-operate" type light and must be depressed to provide the indication.

PARABRAKE RELEASE MECHANISM (Fig 4)

17 The parabrake release mechanism is fitted to the two upper longerons at the extreme end of the rear fuselage. Prior to release of the parabrake, a ball-ended clevis, to which is attached the riser, is retained in an open socket by a cam and release lever mechanism.

18 The cam is eccentric, and revolves about a needle bearing. A cam race, also on a needle bearing, revolves on the cam and retains the ball-ended clevis in the socket when the cam is locked by the release lever. A step machined on the circumference of the cam flange is engaged with a locking pawl on the release lever when the mechanism is in the locked position.

19 The mechanism is arranged so that the load on the ball-ended clevis tends to rotate the cam in an anti-clockwise direction, viewed from the LH side.

20 When the selector lever is moved to the JETTISON position, a pin on the curved arm of the actuating lever pivots the cam release lever. This disengages the locking pawl fro the step on the cam, and allows the cam to rotate and release the ball-ended clevis. A tongue on the cam release lever bears against a lug on the cam to initiate rotation.

21 When replacing the parachute, the selector lever must be in the doors closed position and the master electrical switch OFF. The clevis is inserted in the socket and the cam rotated by hand until the locking pawl engages with the step on the cam. The RH side of the cam is knurled to provide a gripping surface.

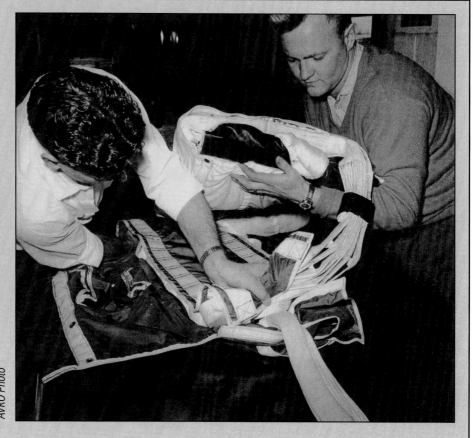

Ian on the left and Peter on the right... with the riser held tight the chute is folded back and forth and stacked into a flat bundle about 1-2 feet high.

AVRO Photo

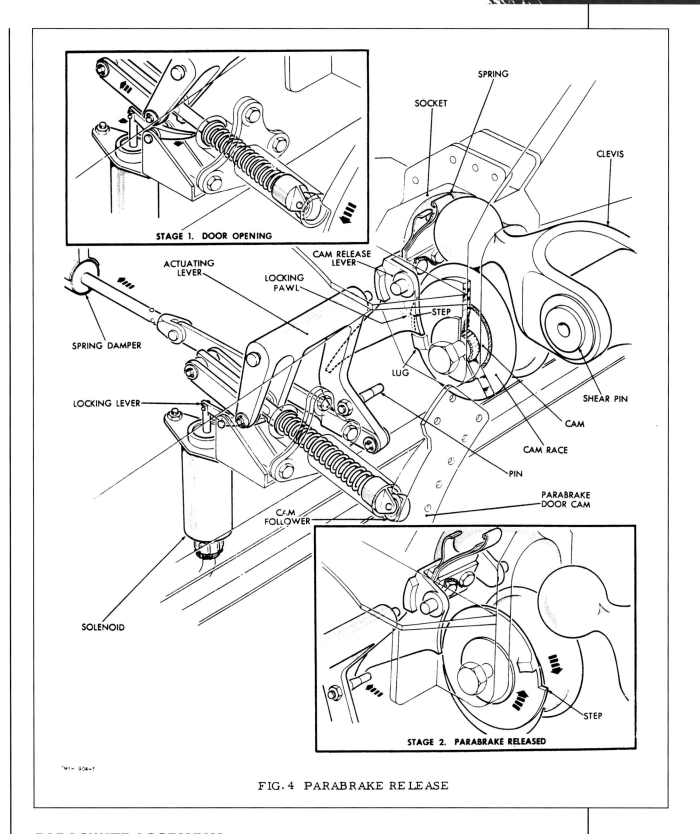

STAGE 1. DOOR OPENING

SPRING
SOCKET
CLEVIS
CAM RELEASE LEVER
ACTUATING LEVER
LOCKING PAWL
STEP
SPRING DAMPER
LUG
SHEAR PIN
LOCKING LEVER
CAM
CAM RACE
PIN
CAM FOLLOWER
PARABRAKE DOOR CAM
SOLENOID
STEP
STAGE 2. PARABRAKE RELEASED

TMI- 904-5

FIG. 4 PARABRAKE RELEASE

PARACHUTE ASSEMBLY

22 The parachute assembly consists of a pilot chute, a bridle line, a deployment bag, a main canopy, suspension lines and riser.

23 The pilot chute is a non-fouling vane type parachute made from Dacron material with a conical coil spring housed in the centre cone of the vanes. The chute is packed in a separate stowage bag with the coil spring compressed.

24 The flaps of the stowage bag are held in position by a steel pin which is attached to the RH door by a loop. See fig 6. Withdrawal of this pin allows the pilot chute to be ejected by the spring action. The pilot chute stowage bag is secured to the upper forward part of the deployment bag.

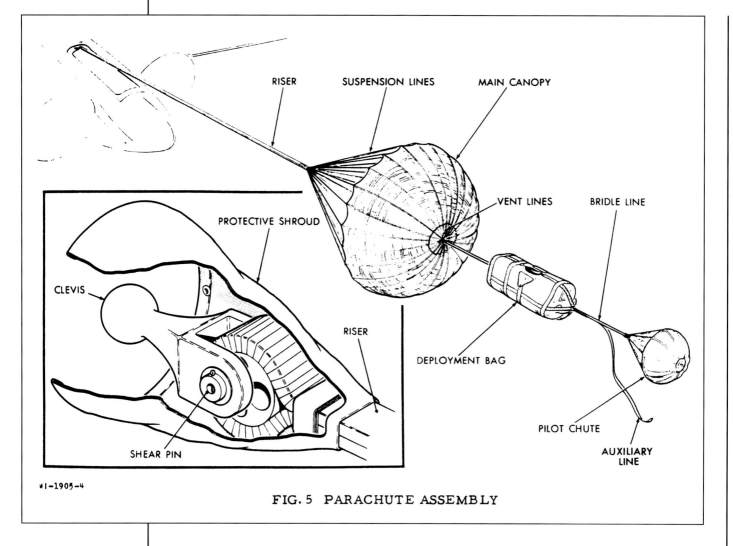

FIG. 5 PARACHUTE ASSEMBLY

*I-1905-4

25 The deployment bag is reinforced by webbing and shaped to fit in the parachute box. Packed within the bag are the suspension lines, bridle line, and the main canopy. The use of a deployment bag reduces the opening shock and provides orderly deployment of the main canopy.

26 A bridle line connects the pilot chute to the deployment bag and the deployment bag to the main canopy vent lines. An auxiliary line, to assist in lifting the deployment bag from the box, is attached to the rear section of the bridle line. The end of the auxiliary line is secured to the lower forward part of the deployment bag by 100 lb. breaking thread.

27 The main canopy is a Fist ribbon type parachute with an inflated diameter of approximately 16 feet. It is made up of panels of Dacron material constructed in a horizontal, vertical and radial pattern. The horizontal and radial ribbons are two inches wide and the vertical ribbons are 5/8 inches wide.

28 The twenty-four suspension lines and vent lines are manufactured in continuous loops of tubular Dacron webbing. The lines are bound together to form the riser which is twenty-three feet long.

The riser terminates in a loop bound around a hardened steel bush which is secured to the clevis by a shear pin. In the event of inadvertent release of the parachute in flight, the excessive load will cause the pin to shear and release the parachute assembly. A protective shroud attached to the riser covers the clevis and shear pin.

29 When the selector lever is moved to STREAM, the door is released and the door opens, withdrawing the pin from the pilot chute bag. The conical spring then ejects the pilot chute into the airstream where it inflates and pulls the deployment bag from the parabrake box. The auxiliary line on the bridle line lifts the rear end of the bag from the box and the 100 lb. thread breaks. Tension on the riser opens the deployment bag and withdraws the suspension lines and main canopy which then inflates and applies the braking load to the aircraft.

30 On completion of the braking run the selector is moved to JETTISON. This allows the cam in the release gear to rotate and release the clevis from the socket, disconnecting the complete parachute assembly from the aircraft, all components being retained with the assembly.

126

TESTING AND SERVICING

GENERAL

31 When carrying out the rigging procedure or checking the cable tension of the parachute brake control cable, the aircraft should be supported by the landing gear and standing on firm, level ground. The instrument pack must be removed to gain access to the turnbuckle and control cable in the armament bay. As the cable tension is adjusted for ambient temperature, the aircraft should be allowed to stand in an even temperature for approximately 12 hours prior to taking tension readings. See Arrow I Service Data - Section 1 for aircraft stability with the instrument pack removed.

TENSIONING THE CABLE

32 To tension the cables proceed as follows:

(a) Set the parabrake selector lever to the doors closed position.

(b) Remove the forward access panel from the LH console in the front cockpit. Adjust on the tension regulator to remove any slack in the cable between the selector lever and the tension regulator. Check that the adjustment plug is in safety and wirelock.

(c) Slacken the turnbuckle until there is no tension on the cable.

(d) C h e c k that the total compensation range of 3. 75 inches can be obtained by applying a tension of 30 lbs. to the output cable and measuring the extension.

(e) Fit a tensiometer on the cable and adjust the turnbuckle in the armament bay until the required tension is obtained. Check that the turnbuckle is in safety and wirelock.

TESTING THE CABLE SYSTEM

33 To ensure that the system is operating correctly, carry out the following function test:

(a) Check that the master electrical switch is OFF and set the selector lever in the closed position.

(b) Fit the clevis in the socket, and rotate the cam clockwise, viewed from the LH side of the aircraft, until it locks. Check that the clevis is securely engaged.

(c) Close the doors and check that the door lock is engaged. Do not connect the pin on the RH door to the pilot chute release pin.

(d) With an assistant in the front cockpit, move the selector lever to STREAM, and check that the doors open freely and fully, and that the clevis is still securely engaged.

(e) With tension applied to the clevis, move the selector lever to JETTISON and ensure that the clevis disengages satisfactorily.

AVRO Photo

The chute is packed into a holding bag, the pilot chute is folded on top before it is pinned shut, the riser fitting extended, ready to be re-inserted into the rear stinger compartment. Many chutes have survived. They are available for modeling any remake.

ARROW 1 SERVICE DATA

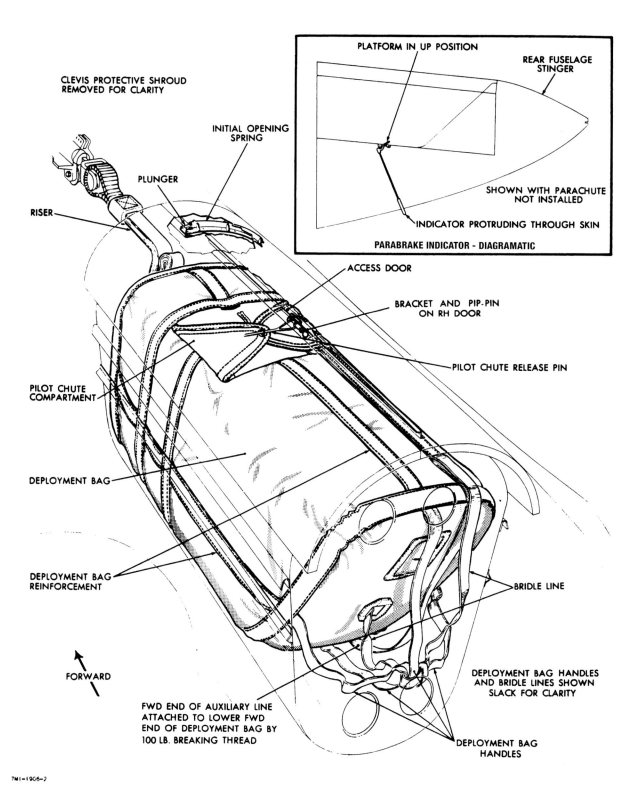

PLATFORM IN UP POSITION

REAR FUSELAGE STINGER

SHOWN WITH PARACHUTE NOT INSTALLED

INDICATOR PROTRUDING THROUGH SKIN

PARABRAKE INDICATOR - DIAGRAMATIC

CLEVIS PROTECTIVE SHROUD REMOVED FOR CLARITY

INITIAL OPENING SPRING

PLUNGER

RISER

ACCESS DOOR

BRACKET AND PIP-PIN ON RH DOOR

PILOT CHUTE RELEASE PIN

PILOT CHUTE COMPARTMENT

DEPLOYMENT BAG

DEPLOYMENT BAG REINFORCEMENT

BRIDLE LINE

FORWARD

FWD END OF AUXILIARY LINE ATTACHED TO LOWER FWD END OF DEPLOYMENT BAG BY 100 LB. BREAKING THREAD

DEPLOYMENT BAG HANDLES AND BRIDLE LINES SHOWN SLACK FOR CLARITY

DEPLOYMENT BAG HANDLES

7MI-1906-2

FIG. 6 INSTALLATION OF PARACHUTE ASSEMBLY

ADJUSTING THE ELECTRICAL SAFETY LOCK

34 The adjustment for the electrical safety lock consists of a special screw mounted on a bracket on the selector lever. Access is through a small hole in the inboard face of the lever cover which is normally closed by a plug button. See fig 2. To adjust the micro-switch proceed as follows:

   (a) Remove the plug button.
   (b) Set the selector lever in the doors closed position.
   (c) Back off the adjusting screw until clear of the micro-switch actuator.
   (d) Screw in the adjusting screw to the point when the micro-switch operates.
   (e) Screw in the adjusting screw a further 1-1/4 turns.
   (f) Replace the plug button.

TESTING THE ELECTRICAL SAFETY LOCK

35 To ensure satisfactory operation of the electrical safety lock the following test should be carried out:

   (a) Set the selector lever in the doors closed position.
   (b) Close the parabrake box doors. Do not connect the pin on the RH door to the pilot chute release pin.
   (c) Connect the electrical ground power unit and switch the master electrical switch ON.
   (d) Apply a tension of approximately 150 lbs. in a forward direction, on the cable in the armament bay and check that the doors remain locked.
   (e) Remove the load from the cable and check that the initial movement of the selector lever to STREAM de-energizes the solenoid and releases the electrical safety lock.
   (f) Switch the master electrical switch OFF.
   (g) Disconnect the electrical ground power unit.

INSTALLING THE PARACHUTE ASSEMBLY

36 When installing the parachute assembly in the parabrake box the aircraft must be in the following condition:

   (a) The control cable must be correctly tensioned.
   (b) The master electrical switch must be OFF.
   (c) selector lever must be in the doors closed position.
   (d) The parabrake release must be open.

37 To install the parachute assembly, proceed as follows:

   (a) Install the correctly packed deployment bag in the parabrake box with the pilot chute compartment uppermost and the clevis and riser to the front. Ensure that the bridle lines and deployment bag handles do not become entangled. See fig 6.
   (b) Slide the protective shroud back along the riser to expose the clevis.
   (c) Push the clevis into the socket and rotate the cam clockwise (viewed from the LH side of the aircraft), until it locks. Pull on the riser to ensure that the clevis is secure.
   (d) Slide the protective shroud over the clevis and attach the female halves of the two press studs on the shroud to the male halves on the aft face of the frame at station 803.
   (e) Tuck the spare section of riser down between the front end of the deployment bag and the front of the parabrake box.
   (f) Close the doors. Open the access door . the RH door and connect the loop of the pilot chute release pin to the bracket on the RH door, using the special pip-pin. Close the access door .
   (g) Carry out a pre-flight check. (See para 38.)

PRE-FLIGHT CHECK

38 Before flight the parabrake should be checked as follows:

   (a) Ensure that the parabrake doors are closed and locked.
   (b) Open the access door in the RH door and check that the pilot chute release pin is connected to the bracket on the RH door. Close the access door.
   (c) Ensure that the indicator rod is flush with the lower skin of the rear fuselage stinger.
   (d) Ensure that the selector lever in the front cockpit is in the doors closed position.
   (e) Switch the master electrical switch ON.
   (f) Check that the PARABRAKE LOCK indicator light on the refuel and test panel can be illuminated by depressing the body of the light. The refuel and test panel is located forward of the LH speed brake and the access door can only be opened when the speed brake is IN.
   (g) Close and fasten the refuel and test panel access door.
   (h) Switch the master electrical switch OFF.

In the Arrow Scrapbook, Jan Zurakowski was walking on the wing of RL 201 apparently conversing with someone, or some group, towards the back of the plane. We now know that there were problems with the chute. This sequence of photos reveals the mystery.

AVRO Photo

Jan wants to see for himself why the indicator lamp in the cockpit shows the chute door to be open.

The whole ground crew appears to be involved. This is first flight after all... nothing can be left to chance. The blobs of paint on the large nacelles were temperature sensitive. The extent of colour change related to the maximum temperatures reached on these appendages during flight or taxiing. These were pure titanium... expensive to say the least.

Jan really wants to make sure that all is well in Camelot... he gets right into the act and helps to set the sensor right.

You might recall, that movies of the chute streaming out the back of the Arrow, often showed that it behaved erratically. Peter Bonell told me that the original chute was never really designed for the Arrow. It was designed to recover a high altitude research rocket from a USAF program. It was off-the-shelf and seemed OK for the Arrow. Apparently, the length of the suspension lines compared to the chute open diameter is supposed to be one to one for optimal use. The Arrow chute suspension line was nearly 150% longer. It would bob this way and that, depending on the cross winds and power settings of the engines. Ideally, the chute was to redirect engine exhaust and reverse it to create the braking effect needed because it was too far back, gusting effects moved the chute around, causing the pilot to use differential braking to keep the Arrow pointed down the runway. Shorter suspension lines were tried and indeed worked better.

AVRO Photo

AVRO Photo

Peter Bonell can be seen hanging off the tow motor, with his colleagues, trying different lengths of suspension lines until the chute showed the best stability. Empirical work at its best!

Arrowmania
It will cost millions!
How will you get the money?

Joe VanVeenen

Yes it will be expensive, about 50 million dollars cash. So what! This project is not about money . It is about National pride. We have a celebration, the hundredth anniversary of powered flight, 23 February, 2009. Coincidentally, it is also the fiftieth anniversary of cancelling the Arrow - what a conjunction! What better thing could we do for this event than to bring back Canada's most famous and, still to this date, fastest airplane, our Avro Arrow!

In the summer of 1998, I met Paul LeMay , an Ottawa resident, who wanted to organize a cross-country tour of a full-scale model of the Arrow — specifically the Alan jackson model from the movie. He persuaded Peter Cope and Jan Zurakowski to write letters of endorsement and set up a not-for-profit corporate shell to build the tour around. Unfortunately, he did not complete the project. I think it is a great idea, and I am not going to let go of it. Thank you Paul!

The answer - Arrowmania

The Alliance is planning a cross-country , two year Arrowmania tour that will inform Canadians at large about the Arrow and enlist their support for the rebuild. Visitors can buy the usual gift items including a whole series of books on the subject. They can also immortalize their donation by contributing $50, and have their name printed on

Joe VanVeenen

one square inch of the wooden mock-up's surface. We can raise the $50 million in this fashion. Many families of former Avro employees, there are thousands, are eager to see a testimonial to their work. This is it! Once thousands of Canadians at large have contributed, corporate Canada will get on board. A million signatures and funding will convince government that the project is serious and worthy of support. Timing is everything. We should ask when the strength of the argument is self evident – not before. The vision of our Arrow crossing this country, joined along the way with all sorts of aircraft, gracing our skies once again for a celebration like no other. is a real centennial of flight. We missed the fiftieth... let's not blow the one hundredth!

Putting Arrowmania together with Toronto's Holman Design

When I was promoting the Arrow Scrapbook in the Toronto-area I met Peter Holman, owner of Holman Design, who was involved in a project called "The Spirit of Flight – World Tour." His idea was to have the Arrow part of this travelling exhibit to demonstrate Canadian technology of the fifties. The "Spirit of Flight" tour traces the history of aviation through the 20th century and looked fantastic, at least on paper. Peter's presentation ideas were truly inspiring. I told him what I had in mind for Arrowmania. He jumped on the project.

Holman Design has years of experience and has master-minded, built, organized, transported, raised and struck over 17,000 exhibits and displays. His client list is the who's who of Canada. The recent Titanic euphoria and shows can be traced, in part, to Holman Design's involvement. He knows what a travelling show is all about. Within weeks he had outlined Arrowmania's display, prepared the 3-D renderings that you see, sketched the outlines for the tour and designed a transportable, accurate full-scale, model of the Arrow.

The model is made up in sections like those of the real Arrow, the major difference being, it is split along its length so that it can be transported. The detail they are capable of rivals a Spielberg movie set. The bulk of the Arrow will be made from a wooden frame covered with foam. A smooth plastic skin will be molded over the foam to complete the exterior. Even the rivet patterns can be laid down with a decal transfer system. The real Arrow was built from the outside in... so will the model. All wheel well details, access doors canopies, landing gear will look like the real thing. Soon it will be the real thing!

An artist's computer rendering, top view, of the travelling Arrowmania exhibit.

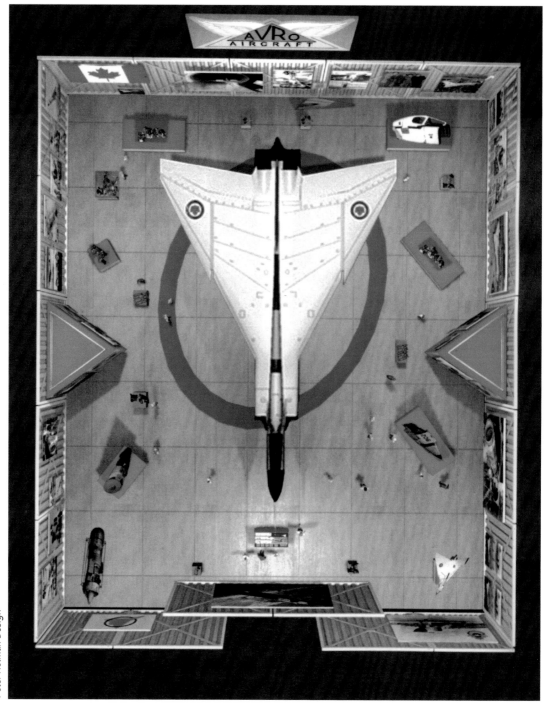

Peter Holman Design

All this activity is not cheap. The model will cost $1.6 million. The tour will cost about $50 thousand per city with 72 cities to go – so about $3.5 million, for a total of about $5 million dollars. I will raise the money through an Arrowmania Limited Partnership. This tax-driven vehicle is a well worn way to raise money for a specific, time-limited project. Investors will be able to write off their contribution against their incomes during the expense part of the tour. When the profits, fund-raising revenues, are counted they will be given back their money and a handsome return for their participation. Come on Corporate Canada and you philanthropists... get on board and help!

The purpose of the tour is to raise awareness and money. There are practical considerations. It would work something like this:

An advance team of two people would visit the town about two weeks before the event, preparing the ground, handling publicity and PR etc. The tour would arrive on the Wednesday night and start setup the next morning. The exhibit would open at 7 - 12 on the Friday night with a formal gala, local dignitaries in attendance and a fifties Rock& Roll party following. For the Saturday hours , 9 - 9, the Sunday hours 10 - 6. Total hours of browsing: 25. The maximum number of people in a limited space is governed by fire laws - about 10 square feet per

The same scene rendered from a different angle to show what it would be like from floor level. It is approximately 15,000 square feet, full knock-down and transportable.

Peter Holman Design

person. Therefore at any one time we probably couldn't have more than about 1,000 people in the 15,000 square-foot overall exhibit. Let's say they stay for an hour; if the space was full all the time (highly unlikely) the maximum number of people through the display in any one weekend would be about 25,000. Let's plan for 10,000 as a workable number.

The number of people who will come forth with their money will probably not be more then the numbers I see in my talks on the Arrow. Probably less, because they won't be caught in the heat of

the moment… say about 20% or about 2,000 supporters per show. If they spend $50 it would be amazing… so total that to $100,000. We need seven times this amount for each show to meet our goal of $50 million. We do have our work cut out for us!

How do we get the rest? Well, one way is to get matching funds from Heritage Canada. Once they see the possibility, its execution and interest they

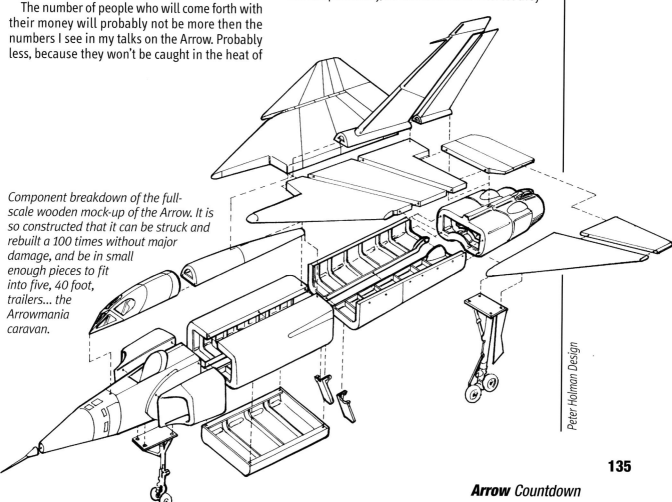

Component breakdown of the full-scale wooden mock-up of the Arrow. It is so constructed that it can be struck and rebuilt a 100 times without major damage, and be in small enough pieces to fit into five, 40 foot, trailers… the Arrowmania caravan.

Peter Holman Design

135

should come on board. Corporate Canada, especially our aviation related industries, unions, and owners could act as another matching partner. After all, this is geared to the 100th anniversary of Canadian powered flight. What I am getting at really is, we will need strategic partners to make it happen. Can you help? More on this later!

The Arrow Alliance can mobilize and inspire Canadian youth.

The Alliance's Arrow Scholarship Program is aimed at young people graduating from high school. The Canada-wide effort to identify an Arrow Scholar will not necessarily require academic excellence but instead will identify the well rounded individual with a leaning to science, technology and entrepreneurship. A $1,000.00 cash award, a one-week wilderness experience and a two-week work term on the national project will set the seed with some three thousand recipients per year.

The Alliance's University Tuition Saving Plan, The Arrow Reliance, is aimed at the discriminating parent/relation/guardian who wants more than just the traditional financial saving plan offered by existing RESPs. Access to educational resources, summer programs & jobs, curriculum counselling, tutoring, educational facilities analysis and access, entrepreneur and career assistance are just a few of the additional services being explored. Savings funds will be invested in educational facilities whenever possible.

Qualified Arrow Scholars will sell the plan. Commissions and administrative fees will pay for participating scholars' education, the national project and related programs. The Reliance will operate as a not-for-profit, recognized charity, able to issue tax-deductible receipts. Arrow Alliance donations and memberships will be actively sought after from government, corporations and individuals alike.

Joe VanVeenen/Peter Zuuring

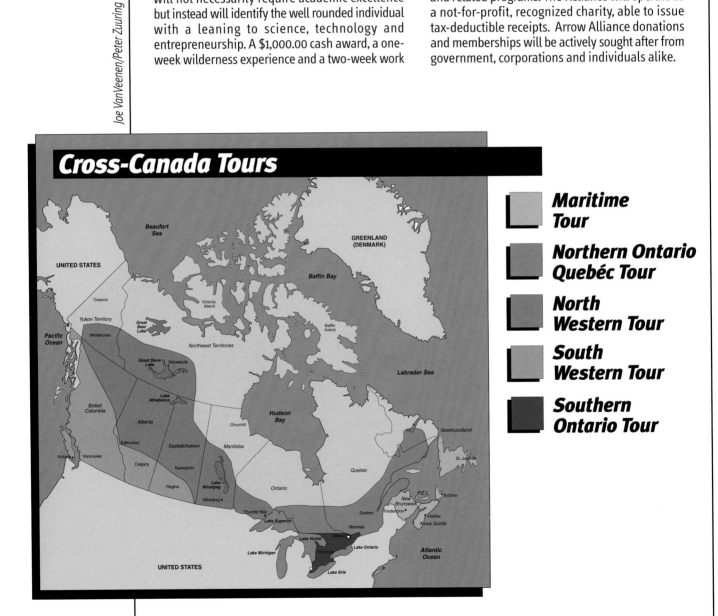

Cross-Canada Tours

Maritime Tour

Northern Ontario Quebéc Tour

North Western Tour

South Western Tour

Southern Ontario Tour

Arrowmania cross-Canada tour, by its sheer magnitude, must be broken down into separate sections. Five tours are planned. The first will be the Maritime section, about 15 cities. It will shake out the bugs and streamline the operation. The Northern Ontario and Quebec tour is next. Following are the Northern and Southern Western tours. Southern Ontario will be the last blitz, since it is the heartland of the Arrow. The whole project will take several years.

The interest in the Arrow is phenomenal. This was clearly shown to me by our website visit report. During the summer of 2000 the CBC ran the Arrow Mini-series once again. I placed two , 30-second adds to see the response of TV exposure. Our hit rate went up five times with a sudden spike, and then a relatively quick reduction back to normal. The hope of Arrowmania is to create a sustained interest which will help see the rebuilding of the Arrow a reality.

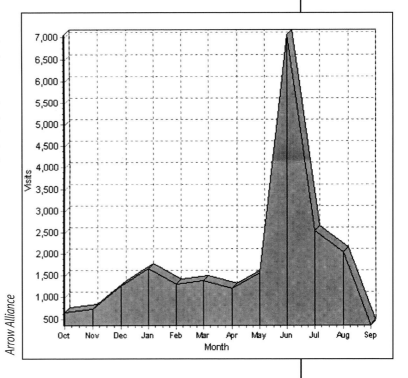

Arrow Alliance

Strategic alliances with other aviation organizations.

Aviation is a huge undertaking in Canada. There are many umbrella groups such as the EAA, RAA, COPA, CASI, CALPA, ACPA, RCAF, Air Force Association, Air Cadets, and Legion just to name a few. They can all help.

Let's use Air Cadets as an example.

The Alliance's goals of leadership and participatory excellence match their objectives. The inspirational aspect and citizenship model are fundamental to building knowledge and responsibility.

The Arrow project can enhance the pride of being part of Cadets. The project can help in promoting membership and highlight the neighborhood participation of the organization. The Arrowmania cross-country tour will give Cadets an opportunity to organize the local event, raise money and host the display. Bringing the true Arrow story home is important to every Canadian because the events that led to the Arrow's demise have not gone away. We should know our history!

The Arrow project can create a spin-off effect that funds local aviation initiatives, expanded flying opportunities and more equipment. Let's use our imaginations.

What if the Alliance collects the funds and fails to rebuild the Arrow?

All funds collected will go into a trust fund to be administered by a recognized national management company such as Deloitte Touche or Ernst & Young. The corporation formed for Arrowmania and the Arrow rebuild will own the rights. Although not-for-profit, the Alliance will control the disbursement of funds through an aviation industry representative board. A nationally recognized legal firm will be engaged to advise on the best way of dealing with these issues.

If, for very good reasons, the Arrow project is delayed or abandoned, funds collected will be directed to promoting Canadian aviation initiatives and enhancing the programs that will already have been a part of the program to that date.

What if the Alliance is successful in bringing the Arrow back?

It will be a great day for Canada and Canadians. It will be talked about for years as the event of the century. It will tour airshows around Canada and the world. It could stimulate a whole generation to really make Canada a place of opportunity, a place to realize your dreams.

Much appreciation...

Jozef H. VanVeenen

Thanks for your continued
creativity and hard work.

Charles Grinyer

"Spud" Potocki

Hank Shoji

Jan Zurakowski

Acknowledgements

David McMillan	ATAC Committee	Storm/Prometheus	Pete Bonell
Peter Bullmann	Heather Kilian	Ken Stevens	Herman Gagné
June Chubb,	Red Wilson	Ken Barnes	Lesley Bruce
John Winship	Bob Pearson	Peter Waddell	André Valiquette
David Beevis	Joanne Brown	Doug Moore	Brian Oakley
Fay McLeod	Jack & Linda Fraser	Ross Richardson	Fleet Aircraft
Jeff Brownridge	G. Bruce	Bob Cairns	Les Wilkinson
Brownridge Family	Frank Harvey	Shoji Family	Jeff Bird
Brian Sabiston	Dan Lajeunesse	John Connell	Elgin Scott

Editorial Staff...
with much appreciation

David Caple
*Vice President and
General Manager
Orenda Engines Ltd.
(1980 - 84) retired.*

Mark Pavilons
*Freelance
Reporter/Editor,
Caledon Citizen*

Lynn Macnab
*With special thanks
for your support and
suggestions*

Essence
Communications Group
*www.essencegroup.com
info@essencegroup.com*

Encouragements

Our Booksellers
Our Museums
Our Libraries
NRC/CISTI staff
Air Cadet League of Canada
Boeing Canada
EAA & RAA Members

Arrow Alliance Membership

Become a member!

Inspiring a new generation by rebuilding the Avro Arrow Complete static display model plus a full-scale flying replica

Individual member
• 1 Scrapbook
• 1 Arrow Pin
• Certificate
• Interactive www-newsletter

Individual Patron
As individual member plus:
• Framed Certificate
• Name engraved on both models for all time
• Arrow Model
• Scholarship Presentation

Corporate Member
• 5 Books/Pins
• Plaque
• Arrow Model
• Sponsor of 1 Arrow Scholarship
• Company Name on plane
• Annual List
• Choose participating school
• newsletter

Corporate Sponsor
• 20 Books/Pins
• Plaque
• Arrow Model
• Sponsor of 10 Arrow Scholarships
• Publicity Package
• Access to Scholars in all programs
• Corporate name and logo featured on plane and all literature
• Newsletter

☐ **Individual Member**
Initial membership $50.00
Annual Renewal $25.00

☐ **Individual Patron**
$1000.00 Life

☐ **Corporate Member**
$5000.00/$3000.00

☐ **Coporate Sponsor**
$100,000/$75,000

The Arrow Scrapbook sets the record straight. Get the real reasons why the Arrow was cancelled. Find out what is left and what we can do about it. Richly supported with period documentation, photos and diagrams. A must for any Arrow enthusiast. **$50.00**

The Arrow cast Bronze Model includes a 1/144 true scale rendition in timeless bronze. Two stainless steel Iroquois engine models are fitted into the tail and slip over two exhaust pipes supported by a detailed cast bronze arrowhead base. Packaged in an aluminum molded case... a true collectors item. Look out for the 1/72 scale version in cast bronze to follow. **$200.00**

Get your name on the Arrowmania wooden mock-up by buying a piece of the Arrow. A small memento indicating your name placement will follow your purchase. If you know someone who worked on the Arrow, what better memory and testimonial than to have his or her name on this timeless Canadian icon. **$50.00**

Order Form *(Please photocopy and mail)*

Name: _____

Address: _____

Tel:Fax: _____

E-mail: _____

Date: _____

Signature: _____

Membership	Amount
☐ Individual Member ☐ Individual Patron	
☐ Corporate Member ☐ Coporate Sponsor	

Item	Quantity	
Arrow Scrapbook		
Arrow Bronze Model		
Buy a Piece of the Arrow		

Total Amount $ _____

Payment Options

☐ Cheque ☐ Money Order
Please make payable to the "Arrow Alliance."

62 North Street, Kingston, Ontario K7K 1J8 Phone/Fax: (613) 531-4156
E-mail: director@arrow-alliance.com • arrowz@attcanada.ca

Thank you for becoming a member of the new Arrow Alliance. Items are in production and will be available as soon as possible.
The Arrow Alliance gratefully accepts any and all donations of an intermediate nature. Tax receipt status pending.

On the Road to Discovery
Finally I meet Sam Lax, the man who scrapped the Arrow.

How did Sam Lax end up at Avro and in the preferred position of scrapping the Arrow programme remains?

During the Second World War, Sam was enroute to Buffalo, NY, on metal business. A freak winter storm reduced visibility and worsened driving conditions. Sam helped a stranded man out of the ditch. This man was Walter Deisher, president of Fleet Aircraft located in Fort Erie. Sam's good deed was rewarded with a scrap contract at Fleet and an eventual position on the Board. Not bad!

Avro's Sir Roy Dobson hired Deisher to be the new president of A.V. Roe Canada Ltd just after the war. It appears that Sam's fortunes would follow Deisher's. Sam started to haul scrap from Avro/Orenda before, during, and after the Arrow programme. He was in the best position to get the Arrow contract with Crown Asset Disposal Corporation, having been there for years and trusted. Sam's secret? He freely showed them his books and his profits on any deal. The Crown had confidence in him!

It took Sam, and 13 other men, three months to scrap what had taken, 14,000 men and women, 6 years to create!

Peter Zuuring with Sam in his Samco Steel offices in Hamilton Ontario. Late in life, and stroke survivor, Sam, somewhat feeble, continues his business interests all the same.

80 Brant Street in Hamilton, now in the hands of Slater Steel, was the home of Sam Lax's operations. Arrow scrap came here. Rumours abound that stuff did get away... we keep looking and hopefully will find it!

SLATER STEELS
HAMILTON SPECIALTY BAR DIVISION
SCRAPYARD
SEE YARD PERSONNEL FOR DUMPING INSTRUCTIONS
80 BRANT STREET